Morris R. Bogard has taught communication and served in various administrative positions at State University of New York College—Cortland, where he is presently Associate Vice President for Academic Affairs. Dr. Bogard has been a communication consultant for several federal agencies and industrial organizations.

THE MANAGER'S STYLE BOOK

Communication Skills to Improve Your Performance

Morris R. Bogard

A SPECTRUM BOOK   Prentice-Hall, Inc., *Englewood Cliffs, New Jersey*

Library of Congress Cataloging in Publication Data

BOGARD, MORRIS R
   The manager's style book.

   (A Spectrum Book)
   Includes bibliographical references and index.
   1. Communication in management. 1. Title.
HD30.3.B64   658.4′5   79-10765
ISBN 0-13-549204-1
ISBN 0-13-549196-7 pbk.

A SPECTRUM BOOK

10 9 8 7 6 5 4 3 2 1

Printed in the United States of America

PRENTICE-HALL INTERNATIONAL, INC., *London*
PRENTICE-HALL OF AUSTRALIA PTY. LIMITED, *Sydney*
PRENTICE-HALL OF CANADA, LTD., *Toronto*
PRENTICE-HALL OF INDIA PRIVATE LIMITED, *New Delhi*
PRENTICE-HALL OF JAPAN, INC., *Tokyo*
PRENTICE-HALL OF SOUTHEAST ASIA PTE. LTD., *Singapore*
WHITEHALL BOOKS LIMITED, *Wellington, New Zealand*

For
NORMA
LARRY
SCOTT
PETER
KEN

CONTENTS

Preface   **ix**

Acknowledgments   **xi**

ONE
A Credo and Working Method   **1**

TWO
Nonverbal Signs and Signals   **17**

THREE
Listen Effectively   **35**

FOUR
Overcome Barriers Caused by Sex, Age, and Race   **43**

FIVE
Preparation = Confidence   **69**

SIX
Organize Ideas   **75**

SEVEN
Use Effective Language   **85**

EIGHT
Delivery = Comprehension   **91**

NINE
Group Leadership and Discussion Methods   **105**

TEN
Interview with a Purpose   **125**

ELEVEN
Write to Be Read   **153**

TWELVE
The Semblance of Style   **163**

APPENDIX
Note on Trustworthiness   **173**

INDEX   175

PREFACE

The purpose of management in any organization is to facilitate productivity. In education, management serves teaching and learning; in government, it promotes efficiency and economy; in business, it stimulates increased development of technology and competence in executing assigned tasks. The manager must maintain credibility with all those with whom he works, both up and down the line of organizational structure.

Although management is an honorable profession and has been made increasingly complicated by new technology and expanding demands of its constituencies, it must never become an end in itself. Management must not be permitted to become a self-perpetuating institution whose sole purpose is to guarantee its continued existence through manipulation of those very elements which brought about its inception.

Because management has as its primary purpose efficient productivity, it logically follows that managers must be able to recognize and to communicate needs and desires, and to motivate activities. An efficient manager is often described as "someone who listens to me," "someone who is always prepared," "someone who is sympathetic and understanding," "someone who lets me know what he thinks," "someone who respects my opinion," or "someone who is really concerned about my welfare and my contribution, both within and outside the organization." Good managers are reliable, energetic, knowledgeable, and caring.

All of these phrases are synonymous with the good communicator, who is someone skilled in research, observation, and various methods of information retrieval; skilled in organization, analysis, and synthesis of material; and especially skilled and creative in the presentation of that material to others.

When a manager can present material to others—whether in an interview, at a meeting, or in some other formal or informal situation—and be reasonably assured that he has been heard and understood, he can also be confident that appropriate reaction and action will ensue that in turn will increase understanding, morale, and efficiency within the organization.

Through effective communication, managers are able to force realistic discussions of issues, to confront and allay anxieties caused by rumor, to unmask half-truth and suspicion, and, as a result, promote full participation and support among the various constituencies that management serves.

The Manager's Style Book provides theory and technique, stated in simple and direct language. It is for middle-management personnel who work in municipal, state, and federal government, in industry, or in education, and it will, if put into practice, help create a management style that is both attractive and effective. The behavior of most people is directly related to what they see, hear, and read; therefore, stress is placed upon acquiring skill in interpreting nonverbal messages, cultivating efficient listening habits, and developing effective writing skills. Because plan and control are the foundations for good communication, sections on organizing ideas and choice of appropriate language are incorporated as prerequisites for a discussion of public presentation. Managers are required to participate in a variety of interpersonal communication situations; therefore, this book considers style and form in interviewing, discussion methods, and conference leadership, and understanding and overcoming barriers to communication caused by race, sex, and age. Techniques for saving managerial time and energy, elements that must be controlled and conserved for efficient and appropriate use, are threads which bind the fabric of this text. *The Manager's Style Book* defines the means of communication in a managerial context and offers suggestions for developing and refining communication techniques.

Should the reader conclude that much of the advice in this modest book seems familiar, or is merely good "common sense," the author will readily agree. However, what is said may serve the reader, as it has served the author, as a reminder of good practices previously learned or understood but often neglected during daily managerial operation.

ACKNOWLEDGMENTS

I am indebted to Professors Maurice Schmaier, Fraser Stokes, and William Hopkins for their interest and assistance in editing early drafts of the text. For the sustaining encouragement provided by Whitney Corey, Richard Jones, Selby Gration, Bill, Norb, Rich, Tom, George, and many others with whom I have discussed the ideas of this book, I am grateful.

Special acknowledgment is made to Gloria Blixt, Linda Pedrick, Em Francis, and Eunice Greenwood for their assistance and typing of the manuscript.

Undoubtedly material is borrowed from some sources without due credit. For such material, I ask the pardon of the authors and offer them my thanks. Many years of reading, teaching, consulting, and practice as an administrator in higher education have developed and merged concepts, precepts, and application of the art of communication so that they have become integrally mingled.

A CREDO
AND
WORKING METHOD

Chapter One

Excellence in administration is something each of us can recognize but few of us can reduce to words. The reason for this is that superior management is not fully defined by methodology and philosophy, any more than is excellence in the performing arts. Management, like any other creative art, involves aesthetic appeal, recognition of human values, a sense of humor, and a highly developed sensitivity to people's needs. Management involves a transaction between individuals, a process whereby values are tested and models of intellect and models of content are compared and evaluated—all within a delicate aesthetic membrane that almost defies analysis. The transactional process in which management and subordinates participate modifies and refines both. Having said the above, I also conclude that as an artist understands the mechanics and properties of the medium with which he works, so, also, must a manager master his technology and refine his style.

Specialized systems for organizing, problem solving, synthesizing, questioning, and interviewing, and skill in small group discussion, along with an acquired sensitivity to values and needs, are all useful tools that provide the manager flexibility in defining goals and precision in application of acquired knowledge and skills. Yet his possession of all of these does not guarantee successful administration any more than the best golf clubs guarantee a score in the seventies, or the best paint and brushes guarantee an artistic masterpiece. It is rather style, as exemplified by behavior, that more clearly defines excellence in administration.

Style in management, however, not only includes behavior as it is perceived by others within the organization but also encompasses an attitude, a point of view, that underlies and motivates that behavior. The most obvious manifestations of style appear in management's interaction with others in the organization, and the most obvious projection of that style emerges in management's communication with other organizations. Although a manager's style tends to be a personal and individual aspect of behavior, its structure depends upon a variety of carefully chosen, tested, and proven communication techniques.

SELF-PERCEPTION

The following exaggerated, hypothetical example of ineffective management style illustrates a complete breakdown in communication because of inappropriate techniques and faulty self-perception. A friend of mine who had his first appointment with the director of his organizational unit arrived on time and was informed by the director's secretary that the gentleman was busy and that my friend could wait in the outer office until the director was available. My friend concluded from the darkened light buttons on the secretary's telephone that the director was not occupied in telephone conversation. When the secretary finally opened the door to admit my friend to the inner office, he further noticed that the director had been alone for the fifteen or twenty minutes that he had been kept waiting. After the secretary ushered my friend into the office, the director invited my friend to sit in the small "visitor's chair" opposite an impressive desk and executive chair. In this chair the director remained seated, swiveling from side to side. Without apologizing for keeping my friend waiting, the director offered his formal handshake, across the desk, and began the conversation.

Two or three times during the conversation, the director completed statements my friend had initiated and accepted telephone calls. At the conclusion of the conversation, the director thanked my friend for coming to the office and bade him farewell, saying, "We will talk again," without rising from his chair.

This story describes a manager whose self-importance and lack of concern seriously impair his style. Some managers really believe that such behavior is appropriate. These managers have been so deluded by the deference others have paid them, because of their position as managers, that they fail to recognize the communication barriers nonverbal signals can create. Such managerial bores use position and status to reveal their contempt for human individuality and dignity. Too few managers realize that a pompous style, characterized by poor manners and a lack of concern, creates antagonism and other communication barriers that are absolutely counterproductive.

Good managerial communications style projects concern through punctuality, succinctness, and good organization; it is alive with ideas and promotes opportunity for response, for it follows the precept that genuine communication occurs when response to the manager's initiation of stimuli is in turn received and interpreted by management. Volume, mass, and position do not connote quality and must not be used as substitutes. The inept manager, in his interpersonal communication, is rude, drones on monotonously, and utters predictable bromides and company jargon, without concern for the reaction of others. He is only interested in "getting the word" to subordinates.

SUPPORTIVE ENVIRONMENT

As a first step in establishing a positive managerial style, the efficient manager institutes obvious and clear lines of communication and takes advantage of informal communication within the organization; he makes openness and receptivity a principal characteristic of his behavioral style. The formal lines of communication established by an organizational chart require a "chain of command" system of communicating up and down the line. This system is recognized by all members of the organization, and its effectiveness is directly dependent upon the quality of input and how well members of the organization adhere to the system.

Informal communication usually consists of techniques that have arisen through the peculiarities of the organization or the behavior of individuals within that organization; these techniques are sometimes much more effective in information dissemination than are the established systems. Most systems of informal communications have simply become precedent or "the way we do things." Some of the most effective informal communication is simply gossip, and frequently it has much more to do with how people "feel" about the organization than does official communication. On the other hand, informal communication is often unsubstantial and illogical, and bypasses the formal systems, which may result in destructive and counterproductive attitudes and behavior.

Openness

In order for management to eradicate or at least diminish destructive and unproductive informal communication, it must encourage open and clear channels of communication that assure all constituents of full and official information about practices and procedures, directions, goals, and priorities as these elements affect their performance in the organization. Good management communications style provides and promotes opportunities to react to communication—either through the formal system or other means.

Strong indications that a manager desires feedback, encourages comment and suggestions, and is amenable to change when a proper rationale is presented go far toward enhancing morale within the organization. Everyone likes to feel that he is contributing. All professionals within an organization should be made to feel that "they are helping run the organization" as a result of their suggestions and actions—and of management's direct response to those suggestions and actions. A managerial technique that encourages openness must also expect negative feelings to be expressed. People who express negative feelings should never be the object of reprisal.[1]

The Personal Touch

That management encourages communication is a sign of recognition to individuals of their worth and potential to contribute. Although personal communication consumes more time and energy, it is much more meaningful than general or impersonal contact. An interview is better than a telephone call, a telephone call is better than a letter, a letter is better than a memorandum, and a memorandum is better than a newsletter.

The manager who personally compliments or instructs someone has both literally and symbolically made a statement regarding that individual's worth and value to the manager—and that recognition will usually be repaid significantly by increased efficiency on the part of the individual.

The most advanced technological systems of information retrieval cannot guarantee an effective flow of communication if the psychological climate within the organization is poor. Good management is concerned with human relations. It is not necessary that everyone be happy on the job in order to be productive (although happiness is a significant motivating factor); it is necessary that people recognize their worth and contribution within the organization and that they not be cynically manipulated through superficial inducements.[2]

Happiness and Appreciation

Job performance seems to be enhanced by two principal motivating factors: (1) the individual must be happy in and with the job he performs, and (2) he must be appreciated. Happiness seems to flow from the environment surrounding the position, not simply from the position itself. Happiness involves recognition of achievement, the challenge and interest of the job, the recognized potential for growth, and the responsibility inherent in the

[1]H. H. Leavitt, "Some Effects of Certain Communication Patterns on Group Performance," *Journal of Abnormal and Social Psychology* 46 (1951): 38–50.

[2]F. W. Taylor, *Scientific Management* (New York: Harper, 1911).

job, and finally, of course, the aspect of recognition and reward for performance well done.

Unhappiness in a job also relates principally to the environment—the physical conditions under which employees work, the repressive policies of an organization, an unsatisfactory supervisory situation, poor relationships with fellow workers, and a general sense of insecurity.

Performance is positively influenced when an employee recognizes the possibilities for self-enrichment through change and challenge and when reward is forthcoming. However, organizational health based solely on constant change and periodic rewards can be self-defeating, for the happiness derived from these artificial manipulations is only transitory; sooner or later the worker will expect another change or reward, and if such is not forthcoming, he will once again be uneasy, restless, and unhappy—and consequently unproductive.

The manager who intends to achieve maximum performance in his organization eliminates jobs that machines can do and organizes the remaining positions that humans perform so that they are challenging, interesting, and responsible tasks; he then rewards those who perform the tasks well. Policies and procedures within any organization must provide clear guidelines for performance so that recognized achievements may be used to promote contentment and job security. Efficient management communication is characterized by sincerity, concern, and behavior that supports those who report to management.

Because of increased opportunities for education and a more affluent society, workers within an organization have been conditioned to expect greater achievement. When achievements do not match expectations, disappointment and disillusionment occur, and a behavior ensues that is counterproductive to the goals of the organization. It is the function of the executive clearly to set realistic goals for his subordinates so that the gap between reality and expectations will not become so wide as to be discouraging.

Handling Values

William Conboy lists seven projected value trends which most workers will seek during the last third of the twentieth century.[3] Conboy believes that organizations and institutions will be evaluated according to how well they facilitate the conditions that these values suggest: *purpose*—the desire to know why; *participation*—the desire to have a voice; *potency*—the desire to have an effect; *protection*—the desire not to be taken advantage of; *pluralism*—the desire to live with alternatives; *privacy*—the desire to be let alone; *pleasure*—the desire to enjoy.

[3]W. A. Conboy, *Working Together: Communication in Healthy Organizations* (Columbus, Ohio: Charles E. Merrill, 1976), pp. 18-24.

Appropriate management style insures that individuals are told not only the what but the why in any assigned responsibility. A subordinate feels more secure and more appreciated when management takes the time to explain to him the logical reason for doing what he is doing and points out the potential contribution that successful completion of the task brings to the total operation of the organization.

Efficient management also establishes networks of communication to insure that participants have a voice in decision-making. When individuals feel that they have contributed toward a conclusion, they are much more apt to support that conclusion than had they not been consulted. Professionals especially take pride in being productive, contributing members of a group. Good managers recognize and take advantage of this. By giving workers a feeling of purpose and participation, management increases their feeling of potency and protection. Potency, if it is not channeled in constructive ways, consistently emerges as destructive or obstructive behavior. When people are ignored—when they feel that they don't matter—they tend to gain attention through unproductive or disruptive activities.

The manager, as the most obvious representative of the organization, must structure a reliable communication system that reasonably assures an environment and a climate in which individuals feel a sense of well-being and security. Only through clear and open communication will this feeling ensue.

Taking Risks

A good manager is not constantly "looking over the shoulder" of those who report to him. He respects them as professionals, he gives them assignments, and then he evaluates their performance on those particular assignments, rewarding them or not as the case may be. The good manager recognizes that different people are stimulated by different inducements, and he takes advantage of this diversity.

Douglas MacGregor's "Theory X—Theory Y Model for Management Motivation" suggests methods of improving productivity in the organization.[4] Briefly, MacGregor contended that management's behavior toward others is governed by what management thinks about its constituency. MacGregor labeled the more traditional management view of what motivates people as Theory X and a more contemporary view of motivation as Theory Y. Basically, Theory X contends that the average worker has an inherent dislike for work and will avoid it if he can; that he must be forcefully directed, threatened with punishment, and strictly supervised; that he really wants direction, wants to avoid responsibility, and seeks security above all else. A Theory X manager feels that the workers do not

---

[4]D. MacGregor, *The Human Side of Enterprise* (New York: McGraw-Hill, 1960), pp. 33–34 and 47–48.

have the imagination or ingenuity to solve work problems; ergo, they are not given problems to solve.

Theory Y managers, on the other hand, take a point of view that work is as natural as play or rest and that indeed it can be a great source of satisfaction. Theory Y contends that the average worker likes to exercise self-control and will work to attain goals; that the average worker wants and will accept responsibility; and that many workers can solve problems, given encouragement to try. Theory Y offers a much more enlightened and informed managerial viewpoint regarding employees.

Although Theory Y is a softer approach to management, it does require specific goals and high expectations for each individual within the organization, and the individual must be evaluated in terms of his ability to meet the stated goals. The Theory Y manager must take some risks in allowing his subordinates to test the limits of their capabilities—to determine their potentialities to contribute. The manager with the Theory Y viewpoint uses error as a learning experience rather than a reason for punishment. Theory Y holds that the internal gratification for having completed a job satisfactorily is a stronger motivation than the external threats of punishment employed in the Theory X view of management control.

Management must respect the employee's right to be left alone. There is no place in a free society for personal data banks and private dossiers compiled without the knowledge of individuals. Recent state and federal legislation has made this practice illegal. Secret information-gathering about personnel must be absolutely forbidden in the organization. When an individual has no privacy, he has no individuality, and when he has no individuality, his motivation and his productivity diminish.

COMMUNICATION SYSTEMS

Good organizations establish systems for finding out the expectations of the individual workers and then set about to tool the management of the organization to satisfy those expectations within the reasonable means and goals of productivity.

Pleasant working conditions, clear communication systems, and a strongly projected program emphasizing the value management holds for each individual worker will significantly promote satisfaction and help to realize the expectations of all members of the organization.

Communication in any organization has two purposes—to inform and to motivate. The effectiveness of instructional communication depends upon organization, clarity, and directness in the preparation and presentation of material. It also depends upon systems to develop, evaluate, and choose the appropriate means of disseminating the information, the timing of that communication, and the special emotional appeals chosen by the

manager to insure the greatest acceptance and understanding of the information.[5]

Motivational communication appeals to pride; it offers incentives for
good work done, and it is structured to establish achievable goals that
enhance the morale of the group. Effective communicators in the organization do not assume that any message is unimportant—is already
known—and therefore is unnecessary to communicate the lower echelons.
Information is important when it is clearly and rationally ordered, and
distinctly presented to those from whom action is expected.

Share Information

Some managers feel that information disseminated from above is for
them only. My advice is to share information with those who report to
management so that each member of the organizational unit knows exactly
what is expected, knows the reasons for those expectations, and may
recognize his ultimate contribution to achieving an outlined goal.

A serious management defect results from an assumption that
privileged knowledge is power—namely, the attitude that what one knows
makes him superior to those who do not know. This attitude causes a
breakdown in the vertical hierarchy or organization communication and
should be addressed and corrected. People in top management positions
must constantly, through a variety of informational sources, check to learn
if information is getting to everyone who needs it. Rewards and recognition
for good dissemination of information are incentives for improved communication. Encouragement provides still more information. Opportunities
to furnish up-the-line communication will short-circuit many gripes and
grievances that may be unknown to management, and problems can be
solved only when management is aware of them.[6]

Circular Response

Too often managers are preoccupied with "getting the word down the
line"; they should spend more time in listening to the word from below. It is
the egocentric and misguided manager who is concerned only with the initiation of the message and not the reaction to it. Although it may be
unpleasant to receive an adverse reaction, mechanisms for receiving both

---

[5]W. G. Bennis and T. E. Slater, *The Temporary Society* (New York: Harper and Row, 1969), pp. 107–124.

[6]For an in-depth study of communication networks, see H. Guetskow and H. A. Simon, "The Impact of Certain Communication News upon Organization and Performance in Task Oriented Groups," in *Some Theories of Organization,* ed. A. H. Rubenstein and C. J. Haberstrow (Homewood, Ill.: Dorsey-Irwin, 1960), and N. C. Daley, "The Delphi Method: An Experimental Study of Group Opinion" (Santa Monica, Calif.: The Rand Corporation, Memorandum RM-5888-PR, 1969).

negative and positive up-the-line communication must be established in order to get all the information necessary for appropriate and productive decision-making.

Just as it is important to disseminate and receive material up and down the organizational communication network, so also is it important to give and receive information horizontally among agencies and personnel on the same administrative levels. To reduce the psychological motivation for competition among equals, the manager must clearly indicate—as a matter of policy—his expectations that information will be readily disseminated, that successful procedures will be shared, and that all agencies will cooperate openly and fully for the organizational good.

The effectiveness of the communication network will be directly dependent upon clarity; ambiguous information fed into the network will result in endless discourse, directionless discussion, and wasteful dissipation of time and energy.[7]

Earlier we mentioned the importance of management feedback to the decision-making process. Let's examine, in the next few paragraphs, a variety of systems for getting reactions from subordinates in order to make the most creative and effective organizational decisions.

Grievance Officer

Some organizations appoint a grievance officer. This independent officer has the responsibility for hearing grievances when problems cannot be resolved through normal channels. A grievance officer in an organization saves time and energy because management need not hear all the individual grievances and because individuals with grievances know to whom they can go for a reasonable hearing, and it is hoped, some action regarding the real or imagined grievance.

Ombudsman

The ombudsman is an officer whose function is similar to that of the grievance officer. The ombudsman serves more independently from management than does the grievance officer, and indeed he may initiate a grievance against management on behalf of employees when he ascertains that a wrong has been committed or a practice is unfair. The ombudsman's position must be filled by an individual of prestige and previous achievement who has credibility with both management and lower echelons. Although he is not a tool of management, the ombudsman can perform a valuable service in gathering information that can assist in identifying and satisfying needs throughout the organization.[8]

[7]Leavitt, *op. cit.,* pp. 38–50.
[8]S. B. Anderson, ed., *Ombudsman for American Government?* (Englewood Cliffs, N.J.: Prentice-Hall, 1968).

Feedback Agent

The time has long since passed when it was appropriate for management to have a "spy" in the communication network. However, many organizations do employ an individual, sometimes a professional management consultant, who is recognized as a representative of management and is responsible for gathering information throughout the organization and regularly reporting that information to management. Such an individual must be very special, for he must be able to reassure the lower echelons that he will not identify them as complainers and that although he is a management representative, his function is honestly and clearly to communicate to management the feelings of those who may be reluctant to use other channels of communication. He must be able to reassure individuals that what they say to him will remain confidential. He must demonstrate that what they say to him influences management policies or procedures. To maintain two-way credibility, he must provide information that is clear, accurate, and free from personal interpretation, so that appropriate changes, if the evidence warrants, will be made.

When the right individual is chosen as a consultant, he can change many feelings that lower echelons have about management by providing subordinates with information, criticism, and innovative techniques that make their performance more productive and their feelings about management more affirmative. Such a consultant must never be used to gather information for the purpose of disciplining another individual within the organization; should this technique ever be employed, all future attempts to use it will lose credibility and effectiveness.

In my capacity as a consultant to various organizations, I have confirmed that members of an organization are less reluctant to discuss problems with an outsider than with someone from inside the organization, especially if positive changes result from the consultation or if those consulted perceive the consultant as one who has "clout" in the organization—that is, influence upon management. I have also noted that members of an organization will much more readily accept criticism from an outsider than from someone within—someone whom they see and work with each day. Consultation, especially criticism, should be conducted in private, one-on-one sessions. Criticism should be positive, reinforcing the affirmative and suggesting methods of modifying techniques or eliminating procedures that interfere with clear communication and effective performance of assigned tasks.

Some organizations use a feedback agent who is a member of the group from which management desires information. Frequently, when this individual is chosen, he is suspected by his colleagues of being the "company man," and therefore candor diminishes. He also is uneasy about his function and his "loyalty" to his group, and therefore often does not reveal the entire situation.

Open Door

Although the "open door" management policy may signal a receptive attitude and a willingness to communicate with all, it is also a time-consuming, energy-sapping operation. Screening by an astute secretary or assistant of requests for appointments will do much to promote the concept and feeling of the "open door" while freeing the administrating officer from having to hear each individual complaint or suggestion. Should a person insist on seeing the manager, take time to see him, should you judge that his problem cannot be handled by anyone else.[9]

Telephone

The telephone is a communication tool that must also be controlled, or it will control the manager. Most of the principles contained in the chapter on interviewing apply to the use of the business telephone. However, because indiscriminate use of the telephone can be a bane of administration, we should examine its useful function when we consider managerial style. The manager who permits the telephone to be an immediate link between thought and action encourages his subordinates to think that the arrival of every idea—no matter how poor—is an emergency. He permits equals and subordinates to direct the use of his time, energy, and thoughts.

A manager cannot possibly keep to his schedule unless he requires that each individual idea submitted be the result of analysis required in the writing of a memorandum, or the planning necessary for discussion. The time it takes someone to make an appointment and walk from his office to the manager's is also time for reflection that may reduce the sense of crisis the caller feels when the telephone is available for easy communication.

Although good management style projects openness and receptivity, the thoughtful manager will seldom return an unexpected phone call unless the caller has left a message that convinces the manager that a real problem exists that only he can handle. As a manager, I am constantly amazed at how many problems resolve themselves and how many solutions are implemented when the passage of time creates pressure for action from an individual who has authority to make decisions.

Efficient use of the telephone demands that the manager set aside a period of time during each day when telephone calls are made and returned.

[9]S. D. Black and A. G. Decker, "Building Good Human Relations," *Management Men and Their Methods,* ed. L. J. A. Villalon (New York: Funk and Wagnalls, 1949), pp. 172–180.

Experienced managers must know what kinds of questions to ask, how to listen and react, and how to budget time for other projects. Business telephone conversations are not the occasion for the exchange of extended pleasantries, although cordiality is important in maintaining morale. The telephone is a quick and easy form of communication, but effective management style regulates its use through an attitude which promotes maximum efficiency.

Rap Sessions

Communication time and executive energy can be conserved when every few weeks the manager sets aside two or three well-publicized hours in which he invites subordinates to his office or to a special meeting room to discuss "what's on their minds"—that is, what's troubling them or what suggested changes they feel are in order. This ventilating process should be conducted in a manner that encourages the most open and forthright discussion. The manager would be wise to have other department heads at this session because their expertise will be valuable in answering questions that may arise. No manager has sufficiently encyclopedic knowledge to anticipate and to handle appropriately all questions. Also, subordinates may wish further management confirmation or interpretation of policies and procedures that have been communicated to them by department heads. Management should take advantage of this opportunity to clarify—not to "second guess" or to overrule department heads. Agreement about what has been said previously and what information will be forthcoming at the meeting must be firm and understood by the entire management team. The purpose of the session is not for management to provide information (although if information is readily available, it should be provided); the purpose is rather to listen, and if immediate answers are not available, to promise future action or information.

Effective Competition

Some managers employ the technique of competition for gathering information or solving a specific managerial problem by appointing two committees or two people to do exactly the same job.[10] The committees or individuals are charged separately and told that they will be expected to provide separate reports and that management will, from these reports, draw conclusions about appropriate action to combat the specific problem. Although duplication may ensue, competition and the fact that more minds are working on the problem often result in a finer, more thoughtful report. Duplication and repetition are not wasteful techniques if the result is a superior product.

[10]Conboy, *op. cit.*, p. 38.

When two such committees are appointed, each group should be told exactly what management intends it to do; that management's conclusions will probably represent a synthesis; and that management will value and weigh the contributions of both committees.

Ad Hoc Special Problems

I recommend that the appointment of dual committees be on an *ad hoc* basis; that is, committees should be appointed for a specific task and abolished when that task is completed. Committees have a way of perpetuating themselves, of establishing policies and procedures that tend to stagnate.

The *ad hoc* committee is analogous to a theatre production, wherein a variety of resources, skills, and talents are brought together for a specific job. That task done, the curtain comes down, the production is dismantled, the results are criticized and evaluated, and personnel are freed for other tasks. Creative action by an *ad hoc* committee results when members of the committee and management are reasonably satisfied that they have accomplished the mission assigned. The *ad hoc* committee has the additional advantage of allowing management the opportunity to select the best people for an assigned task and thereby overcoming "bottlenecks" that may be present in the organizational communication chain.

Rumor

The efficient manager utilizes any effective system that he can, including "the grapevine," to gather information in order to maintain the kind of fluidity, diversity, and creativity that prepare him to meet and solve problems as they arise.

In many organizations, rumor is often considered more accurate than an official communication from management.[11] It is therefore wise for management to take advantage of the effectiveness of rumor by developing methods of using it to influence positive action. Most of us realize that the feelings and impressions we have of organizations in which we work are frequently influenced by rumor—by what people feel and say about the organization, by the half-truths, distortions, and expectations they express to each other in hope of finding solutions and explanations when communication has not been clearly expressed by management. Management can assure appropriate input into this informal chain of conversation by constantly maintaining integrity and credibility through clear and open channels, so that official communication will be available to combat the distortions that occur as a result of rumor. To maintain credibility, manage-

[11]G. W. Allport and L. Postman, *The Psychology of Rumor* (New York: Holt, 1947).

ment must accept what is being said without asking who is saying it. Accuracy, not reprisal, is the best answer to misinformation.

Skillful managers employ the rumor grapevine with positive effect by injecting into it accurate information that they wish circulated. This information must be true, it must be verifiable, and it must benefit both management and subordinates.

CLARIFY EXPECTATIONS

Management style and performance are influenced by the information gathered from a variety of sources and by how skillfully the manager takes advantage of feedback. His skill and speed in gathering and analyzing information and in offering thoughtful reaction will enhance his reputation as a fair and concerned decisionmaker. When the manager has gathered information from all reliable sources, it is his responsibility to communicate to his subordinates the reason for any decision that he makes as a result of that information, in terms that are clearly understood and confirmed by feedback. Dissembling, equivocation, failure to take responsibility for action, punishing or disregarding those whose opinions disagree with management and, worst of all, having no system for gathering information; these characterize the kind of managerial style that promotes only confusion and results in inconsistent practices and procedures in the organization. Effective management style promotes success in the execution of duties for which the organization is designed—maintaining and improving productivity and promoting the personal well-being of all members of the organization. Efficiency is the result of planning and control.

PLAN TO CONTROL

Part of each managerial day should be reserved for planning and coordinating managerial goals and responsibilities. The best time to plan is early in the morning, and the best time to evaluate what was accomplished is at the end of the day. Each action must be thoughtfully structured and directed toward the realization of specific short-range and long-range goals.

A manager cannot plan his time until he has timed his plan. By systematically recording, perhaps even using a stopwatch, the number of minutes devoted to completing each task, a clear picture of how time is spent can be charted. This chart of two or three days' work can then be analyzed to direct more expeditious use of time and perhaps to reorder priorities. He may even discover a more economical use of time that will enable him to set aside periods for solitude and physical exercise, which are both necessary for the maintenance of mental and physical well-being. When such breaks are discriminatingly scheduled, they will not create ill will among subordinates. Management devoted to leadership—not simply concerned with "fire fighting," monitoring, or controlling situations—must have a clear sense of purpose and a set of priorities that place and direct ideas and actions in proper perspective. The manager must never permit crucial time and the will of subordinates to control his actions lest he be robbed of the imagination, growth, and multidimensional opportunities that careful planning and deliberate implementation provide.

SENSITIVITY

Management is the art and craft of working with human beings, which requires certain techniques for expressing desires and satisfying needs—techniques that can be learned and must be constantly practiced. Perhaps the least practiced and most practical way to become aware of the "human condition" is to observe life as it is lived—to observe it accurately, analytically, quantitatively, emotionally, and empathically. Observation includes quiet reflection upon the social and cultural activities to which we expose ourselves through reading, attendance at theatre, concerts, art exhibits, and through active participation in causes that promote social advancement. The culturally alert and socially aware manager is more sensitive to the problems of organizational communication because he has a clearer understanding of what motivates human behavior.

NONVERBAL SIGNS
AND SIGNALS

Chapter Two

Infants communicate entirely without words; through touch, warmth, and various emotional and sensory perceptions, others decode a child's many nonverbal signals and recognize and satisfy his many needs and desires. Later in youth we study vocabulary, spelling, grammar, and syntax, and may even learn one or more foreign languages; nevertheless, adults still communicate largely through nonverbal means. We say that we have "good vibes" or "feelings" about situations or people; we form quick and sometimes strong conclusions about people from the way they look, their mode of dress, and from their general carriage and gestures. We make extended speculative judgments about the quality of character of individuals based upon their countenance, aroma, style of behavior, and how we perceive them to "feel" about us.[1]

As children, we were taught that "silence is golden." Silence is never more golden than in the middle of a sentence, or in a dramatic presentation, if the silence is deliberate so that the listener can clearly perceive an attitude, a point of view, or a "feeling" in that silence.

As a director of theatrical productions for the past twenty-five years and as a teacher of various forms of communication, I am convinced that at least seventy-five percent of the effectiveness of any public speech or any theatrical production derives from elements other than the spoken word. In

[1]A. Mehrabian, *Silent Messages* (Belmont, Calif.: Wadsworth, 1971).

a theatrical production we use music, sound, light, shadow, mass, color, movement of characters in space, and the nuances of characterization that actors display through their physical and vocal response to a variety of stimuli. All factors that apply to a successful theatrical production also apply to public speaking and other communication. Always we are influenced by the actions and reactions of others and by the culture and context in which words are uttered.

Think for a moment about the last movie or television production you saw. It is doubtful that you remember very much of the dialogue unless you also recall vivid physical actions and other visual or auditory impressions that reinforced the dialogue and helped you remember it.

Instinctively we tend to trust nonverbal messages more than verbal ones. We believe what we see, we confirm by touch, and, indeed, at times the nonverbal communication may be the only message we accept. This section will help you become more aware of the nonverbal communication that all of us encounter daily and will suggest methods of decoding some of it so that you broaden your perspectives, sharpen your powers of persuasion, and thus become a more efficient manager.

Movement

The nonverbal messages transmitted by our movements, physical attitudes, and facial expressions are reliable indicators of emotional feelings or contemplated action.[2] Athletes train carefully to read the body language of their opponents and study diligently to learn how to conceal their own intentions. Notice the deception used by a pitcher such as Luis Tiant when attempting to pick a batter off base. The many head or body fakes used by basketball player Nate Archibold or football pass receiver Fred Belitnicoff are largely responsible for their great athletic achievements. A baseball pitcher is admonished to make every pitch "look the same," and a quarterback is advised to make the start of every play look like the last one. Many athletes, such as Howard Twilley of the Miami Dolphins or Jerry Sloan of the Chicago Bulls, with only ordinary physical skills have been successful because of their ability to read bodily intentions in others and to transmit false signals to their opponents.

The principal problem with nonverbal communication is whether to believe the action or the word. The effective executive communicates in such a way that his verbal and nonverbal messages say the same thing. Otherwise, he invariably confuses the observer-listener. Albert Mehrabian, in his book *Silent Messages,*[3] confirms the belief that verbal communication

---

[2]R. Harrison, "Non-Verbal Communication: Exploration into Time, Space, Action, and Object," in *Dimensions in Communication,* ed. J. H. Campbell and H. W. Hepler (Belmont, Calif.: Wadsworth 1965), pp. 160–167.
[3]Mehrabian, *op. cit.*

is not reliable unless it is accompanied by nonverbal signaling such as vocal qualities and physical projections of sincerity. In short, it is impossible to ascertain the full impact of a speaker's words divorced from his actions and appearance.

Gesture

Actions do indeed reinforce verbal communication. Recall the last time that someone told you that you did a good job; recall, too, that when he put his arm on your shoulder, or shook your hand, or smiled broadly and nodded his head, how much more meaning the compliment had. Often physical movements and facial expressions totally replace verbal communication. Has someone ever walked away from you without replying or approached you closely, looked you directly in the eye, and shaken his head negatively? Has anyone ever laughed at an idea you've presented or "nodded off" while you were speaking? These substitutions for language are devastatingly clear in their meaning.

Often when we describe something, we gesticulate for effect. For example, when talking about "crested mountains" or "flowing plains," we may make a motion that indicates the topography of the landscape. A man may describe an attractive woman, not only verbally but also by outlining her profile and form in the air with his hands. Nonverbal signals facilitate communication by signaling—through facial expression, hand gesture, or other movement—that we have finished speaking. We also signal in the same fashion when we wish to speak: we may point to another person or hold up a palm for silence. We may extend an upward palm to indicate that it is time for someone to respond. We lean back in a chair after making a point, saying in essence, "How do you react to that? Now it is your turn to speak." Few of us contradict our oral language as blatently as the man I knew who shook his head negatively and said yes. Invariably I walked away from a conversation with this gentleman confused about his reactions to my comments and his feelings about me.

CULTURAL INFLUENCE

Communication is also influenced by culture.[4] Because of the vast cultural differences that influence human development, human beings have a variety of languages and appropriate gestures and expressions that accompany communication in those languages. An Italian or Latin American uses different gestures from an Englishman or Scandinavian. In America, men are taught that it is not manly to reveal one's emotions to others. In France and

[4]E. Efron, *Gestures and Environment* (New York: Columbia University Press, 1941).

Italy, on the other hand, emotions are readily revealed, read, and accepted. The point I wish to stress is that gestures and facial expressions do *not* have universally understood meanings; therefore we must be very careful when trying to read body language and attach meaning to nonverbal communication out of the context of its cultural milieu.

Response

Good communication involves an exchange of ideas; it is not one-way. We share with, or connect with, those to whom we wish to communicate. Whether they reply verbally or just physically, we get feedback that enhances, vivifies, and illuminates our communication.

One must never assume that he has been understood by others until some action has been taken as a result of what he has said.[5] This action need not be affirmative to assure that communication has occurred. All that is necessary is some reassurance that the receiver of the stimuli has reflected upon what was said.

Most nonverbal behavior reveals something about how someone feels about what was said. However, we can translate our impression of that feeling only in terms of our own experience. Gestures, facial expression, and body positions may mean something entirely different to someone else. However, experience in validating reactions will go a long way toward helping one "read" the nonverbal signals of those with whom one wishes to communicate.

Instant Impressions

The quality and effectiveness of a manager's nonverbal communication, and perhaps in the long run his effectiveness as a manager, are influenced by a variety of nonverbal signals: his body size and shape, clothing, gestures, posture, the arrangement and style of the office furniture, and even the behavior and appearance of subordinates. Quality, style, and performance of subordinates in any organization mirror the leadership of that organization. Judgments are made about places and people based upon their appearance and action, and through an interpretation of that action and the manipulation of their physical and human environment.[6] By being more observant and concerned with the behavior of other individuals and how their physical surroundings influence that behavior, one will become more sensitive to nonverbal communication and more perceptive regarding people's needs.

[5]L. Thayer, *Communication and Communication Systems* (Homewood, Ill.: Irwin, 1968), pp. 26–29.
[6]E. T. Hall, *The Hidden Dimension* (Garden City, N.Y.: Doubleday, 1966).

When we refer to verbal communication, we mean words or symbols chosen to express meaning. But different words mean different things to different people, and interpretation and comprehension of the words require reflection. The meaning of nonverbal communication, however, is usually more obvious; nonverbal communication is more vibrant and offers fewer opportunities for personal interpretation. Words convey information, but they may also be used to deceive, to confuse, and to mislead.[7]

EMOTION AND TRUST

Nonverbal communication tends to be more direct, more revealing, and more influential. Verbal language tends to be intellectual; nonverbal language, emotional. Nonverbal communication helps to maintain attention by furnishing vivid visual signals that reinforce attitudes and ideas that have been translated verbally. Therefore emotional reinforcement compels attention, which promotes understanding.

It is even safe to generalize that verbal messages may conceal while nonverbal messages always reveal; verbal messages are informative, and nonverbal messages are expressive; verbal messages are intentional; nonverbal messages are frequently unintentional. How often have we walked away from a meeting, an interview, or a speech with entirely mixed impressions about what was said or was expected because a speaker provided divergent verbal and nonverbal signals.

If given the choice of trusting and reacting to a nonverbal message or a verbal one, we choose the nonverbal invariably. We instinctively know—and these instincts are increasingly affirmed through research[8]—that it is easier to mislead through words than through actions. It is much more difficult to give the illusion of truth through nonverbal means than through chosen verbiage.

A few years ago, an executive I worked with as a consultant for improving management communication had the habit of constantly smiling or grinning. His motivation, whether conscious or unconscious, was a deep desire for acceptance. Such somber messages as, "We are going to have a reduction in force," "Production dictates that there will be no pay raises this year," or "The management staff has established a new evaluation procedure that will require each individual to justify his production in new and different terms," when accompanied by a smile or grin, did not convey sincerity; as a matter of fact, the executive's countenance conveyed to lower

[7]C. E. Osgood, G. J. Suci, and P. H. Tannenbaun, *The Measurement of Meaning* (Urbana: University of Illinois Press, 1957).

[8]J. Reusch and W. Kees, *Non-Verbal Communication* (Berkeley: University of California Press, 1956).

bureaucrats a cynicism and snideness that were totally unintended. Substitution of a facial expression more appropriate to the language choice and the message readily overcame this personal communication barrier.

Another executive in the same organization wondered why his department heads and branch chiefs were reluctant to enter his office for conversation and why he himself always had to initiate any exchange of information. In a videotaped attempt to discover the cause of the problem, we simulated a conference, in which I took the role of a department head visiting this executive's office. When the executive looked at the tape, he quickly discovered that his nonverbal signaling when answering questions was so aggressive and his general demeanor was so formidable as to be positively threatening. This gentleman had always thought that he was "Mr. Warmth"; his nonverbal signals said the opposite. Viewing the videotape quickly motivated him to change his behavior, and I was told six months later that his relationship with his staff members had vastly improved; both he and they seemed to enjoy more frequent conversations and through greater understanding were making better progress toward their agreed-upon goals.

WE SIGNAL VALUES

In any communication situation, there is a constant assessment of verbal and nonverbal communication. We react to people according to what we perceive them to be—how sincere and well-motivated they seem—and the consequences of our doing what they seem to wish us to do. These perceptions continue to be modified and adjusted as individuals interact. Early impressions are of utmost importance, but they should not always be the final measure of an individual or of what he has said. Although we are not always aware of every nonverbal signal emitted by those with whom we have contact, we must remember that the signals we do perceive are used to judge the credibility, authenticity, and value of what others say.

Eye Contact

In his article in the January 1974 *Speech Teacher,* Steven Beebe[9] reaffirmed the opinion that eye contact enhances the influence and credibility of the speaker. Remember the old saying "A man who has nothing to hide can look me in the eye." Maintain eye contact, without staring. Eye contact signals interest and concern and compels attention. Failure to maintain good eye contact permits diversions and distractions and may convey an attitude of antagonism.

[9]S. A. Beebe, "Eye Contact: A Non-Verbal Determinant of Speaker Credibility," *The Speech Teacher* 22 (1974): 21–25.

Direct and prolonged eye contact, although thought by many people to be a sign of sincerity, tends to cause anxiety in some, for they feel that it is too intimate. There is good reason to believe that the person who looks carefully at another individual tends to dominate that situation.[10] Eye contact is the first acknowledged interaction between individuals.

Because interaction includes the total communication situation, involving verbal and nonverbal signals, it is difficult to isolate and analyze the nonverbal elements. By studying carefully the body movement, hand gestures, and facial expressions of an individual, we gain insights into his moods, energy, attitudes, and perhaps even his motives. These nonverbal messages influence the exchange of conversation.

Looking at someone in order to perceive his nonverbal signals does not mean staring, which is intrusive and rude. When we stare, others tend to feel that their privacy has been violated, particularly if we allow our gaze to rest too long upon one part of the body; blatant assessment of the physical elements of another individual can be destructive to further communication.[11]

In American society especially, there are certain parts of other people that we are not supposed to look at. We know that we can look at someone else's face, his body probably down to his breast bone, and from his knees down to his shoetops, but the mores of society lay strictures on our looking at other anatomical parts. In fact, we do look at them but in polite society only fleetingly, and if caught in the act, we pretend that we have not looked.

For good eye contact, study the pupil dilation in your listener's eyes; it is a clear key to his receptivity to what you say. When the pupil dilates, agreement is generally connoted. On the other hand, when the pupil narrows, the individual may nod his head affirmatively and smile, but you can be reasonably sure that he has some doubt about accepting what you say.[12]

Arms and Legs

Arms folded across the body or legs crossed indicate a defensiveness or a protectiveness; they are a signal that the individual is on guard. In contrast, open arms and uncrossed legs generally indicate a relaxed, receptive, and trusting inner feeling.[13] We lean toward people or things we like; we lean away or turn away from things we are ashamed of, embarrassed by, or strongly disagree with. Occasionally we lean forward if we wish to attack an

---

[10]D. Mortenson, *Communication: The Study of Interaction* (New York: McGraw-Hill, 1972), pp. 212–213.

[11]M. Koneya and A. Barbour, *Louder Than Words* (Columbus, Ohio: Charles E. Merrill, 1976), pp. 46–49.

[12]R. Arnagin, *Visual Thinking* (London: Faber and Faber, 1969).

[13]L. Vande Creek and J. Watkins, "Responses to Incongruent Verbal and Non-Verbal Emotional Cues," *The Journal of Communication* 6 (1972): 311–316.

idea or an individual. The "full front" position is the strongest position an individual can take when conversing and indicates the greatest interest.

We might also generalize that the severity of the angle away from the stimuli connotes a diminishing interest or a desire to escape. Nonverbal behavior that indicates an openness and a receptivity is more desirable and therefore should be controlled and utilized, for it establishes a supportive climate conducive to developing stronger personal relations.

Entire audiences certainly exhibit nonverbal signals indicating openness or antagonism to a speaker. These signals directly affect the speaker. Experienced speakers are especially sensitive to the gestures and positions of people in the audience that demonstrate feelings of suspicion, defensiveness, and loss of interest, so that they can constantly modify their own signals and stimuli to reinforce the message and also maintain or regain the attention of their audience.

Careful investigation and analysis of the communication process is essential because usually, the better people know one another, the more they trust one another and the more intimate their relationship becomes. As intimacy increases, nonverbal communication increases in importance and spoken communication lessens. Choosing the correct nonverbal support—that which is most appropriate to the situation and appealing to the participants—is essential for reinforcing trust.[14]

The Visual Code

It would serve no good purpose at this time to discuss at length the "visual code" that was concocted by elocutionists half a century ago and which illustrated, through drawings and photographs, a variety of physical postures and poses intended to connote emotion.[15] Study of these elocutionistic poses would do little more than make one aware that there has been extensive contemplation and theory, and indeed a system of behavior taught, that stressed the importance of body language and gesture as elements of communication.

Effective gestures and body movements must logically grow out of the situation and reinforce the verbal language. Any gestures or body movements that become communication in and of themselves should be eliminated, incorporated as an element of individual style, or carefully retooled to support the spoken language; otherwise they may prove to be distractions. Nothing more than a stilted, mechanical presentation can result from an elocutionistic approach to the use of movement and gesture.

Kinesthetics is the study of how human beings communicate through gesture and movement. Paul Ekman has categorized these gestures as il-

[14]T. Ekman and W. V. Friesen, "The Repertoire of Non-Verbal Behavior: Category, Origins, Usage, and Coding," *Semiotica* 1 (1969): 49–98.

[15]J. W. Shoemaker, *Advanced Elocution* (Philadelphia: Penn Publishing, 1919).

lustrators, regulators, effect displayers, and adaptors.[16] Illustrators complement the spoken word, regulators control interaction, effect displayers indicate emotional states, and adaptors are movements that may have served some instrumental purpose in early life and are continued later as a habit. All of these classifications may be used interchangeably depending upon the context of the situation. The thing to remember about kinesthetics is that one cannot categorize a specific gesture or movement and say that it means the same thing in every situation.

As an experiment, try looking in the mirror to convey an emotion nonverbally. Observe carefully to see whether you are revealing that emotion or concealing it. Better still, ask someone else to practice nonverbal communication with you, perhaps your wife or husband or a professional colleague or friend. Discuss honestly the emotions you wish to convey by nonverbal signals. You will probably discover that you are successful if you stay with the basic emotions, but when you attempt more subtle nuances, you will find a variety of interpretations of what you had intended to communicate.

Empathy

As a theatre director and teacher of communications, the best exercise I have discovered for ascertaining meaning in nonverbal communication is to attempt to empathize with the other individual. In other words, ask, "What would I do if I were in his situation with this kind of stimulus? How would I react? How would I feel inside if I conveyed those nonverbal signals to another individual?" Empathy is the ability to create in oneself the same feelings and emotional state of another individual. When one can successfully empathize, then one may be able accurately to reconcile observed nonverbal reactions with emotional states. In nonverbal communications, some signals are intended and some are not. Control of nonverbal signals enhances one's ability to communicate clearly, accurately, and vibrantly with others.

Interaction

Appropriate nonverbal interaction involves an exchange or a trading of signals. We are all aware of the tendency for individuals to use downward head, eye, and hand movements at the end of statements and upward movements at the end of questions. We have noted a leaning forward or leaning in when we wish to make a point or are particularly proud of a point we have made and a turning away or leaning back when we are unsure, fearful, or doubtful about statements we have made. It is well to be

---

[16]Ekman and Friesen, *op. cit.*

aware of these nonverbal signals in order to know when it is your turn to speak. Notice how, just before the other individual has concluded his comments, we (the listener) begin to react. We begin to signal that we would like to respond—by nodding the head affirmatively, shaking it negatively, shifting position in sitting, raising a hand or finger, or rising from our seat. Usually this last action is taken by those in authoritative positions.

Vibrant conversation is rhythmic in nature; it is synchronized so that individuals have an appropriate and timely opportunity to respond to all stimuli. People who have worked together for extended periods anticipate one another's needs, and thus the rhythm of conversation becomes smoother. The good communicator is conscious of nuances so that he may at times substitute listening for speaking—and receive equal benefit from both. No matter how skillful you may be as a formal public speaker or in directing interpersonal communication situations, you must be equally skilled as a reactor and listener to others, for communication is a constant adaptation to other individuals, to situations, and to the context of the conversation.

PROXEMICS

Edward Hall articulated a theory of communication called "proxemics" in which he contended that space itself communicates.[17] Hall presented ideas that theatrical directors have understood for more than a century. They are fully aware that there is communicative value in spatial relationships among individuals and in their spatial relationship to the environment. A good director controls the emphasis in a scene by "blocking" the movement to make each actor or each idea, or even each word or phrase, *most important* at a specific time. He does this by directing audience attention to that particular idea through planned movement, the characters' positions, light intensity, costume color, and many other nonverbal signals.

Spatial Relations

Buildings can and should be designed, rooms furnished, and offices arranged for easy exchange of ideas, stimulation of conversation, and creative intercourse. Conversely, managers can demand that buildings, offices, and rooms be designed or arranged to provide the isolation necessary for quiet reflection. In designing and assigning space, a manager should carefully decide what he really wants to accomplish through his spatial relations. For example, does he wish to encourage conversation? If so, then he should arrange space that includes common meeting rooms, open office areas, and no architectural features that prohibit or restrict conversation.[18]

[17]E. T. Hall, *The Silent Language* (Greenwich, Conn.: Fawcett, 1959).
[18]N. Vidulich and D. J. Wilson, "The Environmental Setting as a Factor in Social Influence," *Journal of Social Psychology* 71 (1967): 247–255.

Patrice Horne discovered through experimentation that men react more favorably to large and airy work spaces, while women are more comfortable in more closely confined working areas.[19] An important question to ask is "How much space does an individual need in order to feel uncrowded and uninhibited?" Requirements vary from individual to individual and reflect a person's cultural background and psychological needs.

Individuals tend to crowd together when they wish to lose their individual identity and become "part of the crowd." Giving people in authority greater public space is also quite common. How close is too close for comfort? In the United States, a male usually stands eighteen to twenty-four inches away from another male when he speaks. If he is speaking to an unfamiliar female, he generally increases that distance by four to six inches. Females stand closer to one another when they converse. If one male advances to within a foot of another male, he is considered rude, or his masculinity may be questioned.[20] If a male advances within a foot of an unfamiliar female, he is thought unduly aggressive, and he may therefore unintentionally terminate the conversation.

Our need for space depends upon our concept of self, our sex and the sex of others, our race and that of others, our economic and social class and that of others, and our attitudes about those with whom we are conversing and their attitudes about us.

Each person regulates his need for space according to the situation and the person with whom he is interacting. On a crowded bus or elevator, a man may stand very close to a woman if his back is to her; however, if he turned and faced her, both would feel uncomfortable and back away to a "safe distance." One may easily detect spatial needs in meetings when he observes someone place a hat or coat on the next chair or find a seat in the back row or at the far left or far right. In such ways people put space between themselves and others, and violating that space may make the individuals uncomfortable and interfere with communication in that particular meeting.

Space Control

It is much easier to control space when we stand, but most conversation occurs when people are seated. Seating arrangements can encourage or discourage conversation. Waiting rooms in airports, bus stations, and railway terminals are often arranged to force people who desire conversation to adjourn to a bar or restaurant—"where they must pay for their privacy."[21]

Table Talk

When two people converse at a table, they usually take corner positions if possible so that they can make good eye contact when necessary but also look

---

[19]P. Horn, "Newsline," *Psychology Today,* April 1974.
[20]Hall, *The Hidden Dimension.*
[21]K. Little, "Personal Space," *Journal of Experimental Social Psychology* 1 (1965): 237–247.

away without being rude. The corner positions also avoid conflict, psychologically suggested by face-to-face positions across the table. The former place people in closer proximity, reducing the necessity for speaking loudly and making nonverbal signals more easily detectable. The right-angle position at a table is preferable when people are cooperating to solve a problem; people seated opposite each other tend to assume an attitude of competition and unspoken aggression.[22]

Distance

The best distance for general discourse is three to eight feet between individuals. In larger rooms, the distance should be less because in them, distance is magnified and nuances of communication are absorbed by the space. In a small room, a distance of six to eight feet is tolerable because attention is confined by the walls of the room. Conversation should never be attempted between individuals more than eight feet away from one another because the signals are then so blurred by distance that their effectiveness is considerably diminished.[23]

Seating Arrangements

When people are arranged in a circle for a meeting, they more readily respond to the person directly opposite them, and they respond much less to those closest to them on the right and left. It is therefore an exercise in managerial manipulation to arrange the seating in order to stimulate or lessen the expression of conflict; however, a manager may sometimes deliberately place people with opposing points of view opposite one another in order to stimulate discussion. The eye contact made possible by face-to-face seating is the principal stimulation which motivates a heated exchange. When people are prevented from readily looking at one another, conflict tends to diminish.[24]

In formal seating arrangements, the speaker can reasonably be assured that the greatest response will come from a group of individuals seated in a triangle whose base consists of the front row and whose apex is an individual approximately in the center of the room.[25] Individuals within this triangle will ordinarily be the active participants in the meeting; those on the periphery will be merely observing participants. A manager may conclude justifiably that he has not reached or heard from the entire group but only from those within the triangle who are interested and motivated to

[22]R. Sommer, "Studies in Personal Space," *Sociometry* 22 (1959): 250–261.

[23]Hall, *The Silent Language.*

[24]E. T. Hall, "A System for the Notation of Proxemic Behavior," *American Anthropoligist* 65 (1963): 1103–26, and B. Steinzor, "The Spacial Factor in Face-To-Face Discussion Groups," *Journal of Abnormal and Social Psychology* 45 (1950): 552–555.

[25]Koneya and Barbour, *op. cit.,* pp. 70–72.

speak. Perhaps the possibility of a controlled seating arrangement that demands different triangles of participants for different meetings and purposes is worth considering.

Attitudes and Feelings

"Proxemics" describes the distance people maintain between themselves and others as they carry out their daily business, but the theory also includes the use of space in offices, houses, and development of communities.[26]

Physical environment communicates feelings and attitudes. Notice the feeling of quietness and sanctuary you experience in a church, mortuary, or library; conversely, note the feeling of activity, almost a demand for noise, in a gymnasium, nightclub, or brightly lighted cafeteria. Have you ever noticed the behavior of individuals in a pool room? In a bowling alley? Some bars are more successful than others; they appeal because of the "feeling" in the room, which is affected by the general decor, lighting, and attitudes projected by the owner and bartender. Most drinks contain the same liquor and cost about the same, so the success of a bar generally has to do with how we the patrons feel about the atmosphere, the nonverbal communication signals to us that we are welcome and safe and that our needs will be satisfied there.

Proximity and Relativity

When arranging a meeting, it is easy to focus the center of attention by placing one chair, larger than the others, in the most prominent area of the room—perhaps even on a raised platform—or at the apex of a recognizable triangle. As soon as people enter the room, they will know where to look, that the person conducting the meeting will occupy the chair of "prominence," and that the meeting will be rather formal. If, however, informality is desired, avoid designating a "chairman's position" in the front of the room. Individuals are perceived by others to take on the same qualities and authority as the objects with which they associate. The object (chairman's seat) can become a message in itself; it can add to or detract from the intent of the speaker.

The close proximity of other individuals to the chairman, or person who occupies "the chair," is further nonverbal communication of station and status. We hear a person referred to as the "right-hand man" for good reason. We tend to permit and sometimes even demand that close friends sit nearer to us than mere acquaintances. Closeness to power indicates achievement.

[26]Hall, *The Hidden Dimension.*

Shapes and Sizes

It is also worthwhile to consider the psychological implications of variously shaped tables.[27] The square table has four equal sides, but because it has corners that separate the individuals, it suggests aggression or contention. The rectangular table with its four sides presents a unity, but its lines tend to pair individuals; also, the different dimensions of the sides offer an opportunity for one individual to assume leadership by sitting at the head of the table, which subordinates those seated on the longer sides of the rectangle. The round table, with no "head" and no sides, psychologically expresses unity and cohesion.

Architectural design is more than a reflection of an architect's intent, talent, and skill. Style is intended to convey a message or a quality about the institution that occupies the building. It may be designed to convey solidness and durability if it is used by a banking concern. Government and academic buildings frequently are designed to suggest permanence or timelessness; a theatre, creativity and imagination; a gymnasium, activity. We often do business with a concern simply because we are attracted to the building it occupies.[28] Spatial design—the form and mass of objects in that space, and their arrangement—are telling communicative elements; as such, they should be carefully planned.

PERCEPTION

Perception in recognizing the communicative value of space and design has to do with our own taste and our ability to see clearly and to evaluate what we see. This kind of perception is magnified in our daily encounters with fellow human beings. In his article "Looks and Glances," Arthur Ogden writes of "Glances and gestures—the meaningful changes of the human face. . . . They open to us the delightful and hazardous prospect of shared existence. They reveal the presence of other beings, compounded like ourselves of oblique flesh through which run currents of feelings and intentions that are accessible to our sight."[29]

Almost daily, we encounter individuals who are prospective acquaintances and eventually perhaps dear friends. Factors such as eye contact, the sex and appearance of the other person, environment, and the specific circumstances of the situation all come to bear on the brief moment of decision when we meet or avoid meeting the other person.

Often we simply ignore the other person, even though we have been

---

[27]Koneya and Barbour, *op. cit.,* pp. 58–60.
[28]R. Sommer, *Tight Spaces: Hard Architecture and How to Humanize It* (Englewood Cliffs, N.J.: Prentice-Hall, 1974).
[29]A. Ogden, "Looks and Glances," *Harper's Bazaar,* June 1961, p. 109.

concentrating steadily on his or her approach and appearance. It is normal to behave in this way in elevators, buses, subways, and other public conveyances in order to protect our own solitude. It is easier to ignore other individuals in a crowd than in a one-on-one encounter in a hallway.

Should we choose to acknowledge someone, we may look him or her in the eye, smile, gesture, or offer a comment. Usually our blink rate increases to mask our eyes, indicating that we are not looking at anything in particular or being judgmental, and the other individual generally does the same.[30] Should our eyes meet, it is an obligatory norm that we acknowledge the other person. Not to do so would be considered rude.

When we encounter others, we do not hesitate to make judgments about them based on their appearance, posture, and manner of movement before we have ever heard them speak or observed their efficiency or lack of it in job performance. Why is this? It is because first impressions have proven to be very telling, and they are very easy to make. Americans, especially, have enjoyed easy conclusions and have based much of their behavior upon first and fast impressions.[31] The open-minded individual, who desires to develop personally, lets first impressions fade as he comes to know someone better and can assay the depth of that person's personality and the quality of his mind.

Be alert to signals, but also be flexible and remain ready to modify first impressions.

As individuals, we tend to attribute favorable personality traits to people with body shapes that closely approximate our own. A well-toned body that allows an individual to move gracefully and with assurance communicates self-confidence. Good muscle tone is necessary to communicate the assurance and vigor essential to good managerial leadership. In communication, we need constantly to be aware of how our appearance affects others—of the meanings and attitudes they attribute to our gestures, dress, skin color, physical shape, and size—and to avoid the pitfalls of stigmatizing or classifying individuals and expecting their behavior to conform to our preconceptions.[32]

Clothing

Modern men and women wear clothing both because of environmental conditions and cultural factors. We wear clothing to assist us in projecting our attitudes, feelings, and personalities and to convey our awareness of form and fashion. As a college administrator, I note with interest the

[30]*Ibid.*

[31]C. Darwin, *Expressions of Emotions in Man and Animals* (Chicago: University of Chicago Press, 1965).

[32]H. Bosmagian, *The Rhetoric of Non-Verbal Communication* (Glenview, Ill.: Scott, Foresman, 1971).

denim jacket and blue jeans that some fifty-year-old professors continue to wear to show that they sympathize with the humanitarian causes considered radical in the 1960's and early 1970's. This kind of signaling enables these "mature" individuals to gain the attention and acceptance of under-graduate students, especially women, who think them "with it" but would probably ignore them were they twenty years old and more conservatively attired. Blue jeans and denim jackets have become a uniform of protest against "the system," albeit somewhat dated but apparently still successful as a nonverbal communication agent.

Virtually all clothing is a deliberate attempt by the wearer to convey a message. Correct perception and interpretation of that message enhance and enrich communication and may assist someone in conveying a desired impression. On the other hand, should we allow skin color, body shape or size, dress, odor or aroma, or voice quality to prevent us from fully explor-ing the depth of an individual, we have allowed nonverbal signals to deny us full access to the personality and intellect of another.

Body Types

Physiologists have divided body shapes into three categories:[33] the en-domorph, who generally has more flesh than bone; the mesomorph, who is much more muscular and physically well-developed; and the ectomorph, who is tall and frail, with very little fatty tissue and delicately defined musculature.

We attribute different personality traits to these body types. The en-domorph is thought of as good-natured and agreeable, the mesomorph as athletic and adventurous, and the ectomorph as more aesthetic and artistic. The danger, of course, in relying exclusively on this nonverbal communica-tion is that of generalizing about the behavior of everyone in a particular group.

Symbols of Achievement

Quite often people are "turned off" by the symbols of achievement that we parade. They may be so annoyed, in fact, that they refuse to hear what we say; they don't really listen. Managers who drive luxurious automobiles or belong to "the" country club, a fraternity, or some other exclusive organization occasionally must "overcome" these signs of class. On the other hand, the image conjured up by these symbols may, of course, be skillfully employed to convey a desired meaning and position. It all depends on the attitudes and values of the particular audience.

[33]W. H. Sheldon, *Atlas of Man: A Guide for Somatotyping the Adult Male at All Ages* (New York: Harper and Row, 1954).

Odor

The effect of odor, pleasant or otherwise, on communication cannot be denied. Extensive use of perfumes, colognes, after-shave lotions, and other disguises of human body odors is occasionally perceived as a sign that someone is so unsure of himself that he must present the cosmetic fragrance as an introduction. Discriminating selection and temperate application of artificial scent is advised. We should overcome our conditioned value system that draws different and objectionable cultural and ethnic inferences from odors. We should surmount adverse reactions to odors other than those that result from improper hygiene.

Time

Time is also an important communication signal. An individual who is ten minutes late for a meeting with four other people has, in my opinion, wasted forty minutes of time and has shown a disregard and lack of consideration for the other individuals. Time is the single organizational commodity that cannot be recovered, and how people use it is an important indicator of their personality. My feeling about time, of course, is the result of my experience and cultural background, in which "time is money." But my personal background aside, punctuality is surely a virtue that is expected in efficient organizations.

Touch

We should all become more aware of the communicative value of touching someone else.[34] Touching is overt; it is a more powerful form of communication than words and more powerful than exchanging glances. In some situations, touch may serve better than words to express feelings. Status and authority become considerations because the person with the most power is much more likely to initiate the touch. A person in a lower station who initiates the touch might be considered brash. I know one executive who refuses to patronize a very popular restaurant because the host always touched his arm when greeting him.

Some researchers assert that when a man touches a woman other than in an intimate situation, it is an attempt to dominate her.[35] From my observation, the initiation of touch, by male or female, does come from the dominant person.

[34]Koneya and Barbour, *op. cit.,* pp. 50-53.
[35]"A Picture of Power—No Bigger than a Man's Hand," *Psychology Today,* January 1972, p. 26.

Looks and Glances

We will conclude this chapter by reemphasizing that good eye contact is the principal nonverbal interpersonal communicating agent, whether in one-to-one conversation, group discussion, or a formal public speaking situation. The circular seating situation promotes better eye contact because everyone can look into someone else's eyes. Irwin Altman, in his paper "Privacy: The Conceptual Analysis,"[36] contends that "a look can telegraph real or imagined feelings and can invade a person's privacy." A look or glance is acknowledgement that we are aware of someone else's presence. This acknowledgement is sometimes disconcerting; some women have discovered that by staring back at a man they can quickly terminate his scrutiny. An individual cannot look us in the eye when he wears dark glasses or a large-brimmed hat that hangs over the eyes. We immediately suspect that he is hiding something or is ashamed of something. In fact, the surest way to terminate a conversation is to refuse to look at another individual.

---

[36]I. Altman, "Privacy: A Conceptual Analysis" (Paper presented at the American Psychological Association Convention, New Orleans, La., September 1974).

LISTEN EFFECTIVELY

Chapter Three

2049884

Except among the organically handicapped, perception is largely determined by habit. Two different people can listen to a conversation and go away with completely different ideas of what was said, depending on each observer's interest, attitude, and listening habits.

Listening, like other communication skills—such as reading, writing, and speaking—can be improved. There are techniques of listening that one can incorporate in interpersonal communications that will make him a more cooperative, interesting, and vibrant communicator. Remember: communication is a partnership, dependent for its success upon the active contributions of all.

When we hear, do we really listen? The answer is yes—if we are stimulated to active attention. We are motivated to attention when we are vitally interested in comprehending, organizing, and retaining specific information; or we may listen for sheer pleasure.

CULTURAL AWARENESS

We often fail to listen to ideas that do not conform to our own narrow environment and cultural background.[1] This immaturity usually is modified

[1] R. G. Nichols and L. A. Stevens, "Listening to People," *Harvard Business Review,* 16 (September-October 1957): 88–90.

as we become more tolerant through our exposure to a variety of people and places and because of our sharpened awareness brought about through reading, television, and other cultural communication phenomena.

ACTIVE PARTICIPATION

Although passive hearing can offer pleasure, relaxation, and sometimes escape, active listening is more than simply reception of sound. It is the basis for understanding.

Ralph Nichols, in his extensive studies at the University of Minnesota, discovered that after the average person has heard something, he remembers only fifty percent of what has been said—no matter how carefully he thought he had listened—and after a few weeks, he remembers only about twenty-five percent of what had been said.[2] Certain things can be done to prevent this. The initiator of any communication can reinforce, with personal vitality and visual imagery, his oral language in order to make it interesting, meaningful, relevant, and therefore memorable. However, it is also the responsibility of the listener to be receptive and perceptive. Listening requires active participation, an expenditure of energy. Good listening can be as tiring as reading, writing, speaking, or many other, more physical, activities.

Hearing and listening are not synonymous, and there is no direct correlation between intelligence and the ability to listen.[3] Some people who have to work harder to hear make better listeners because they focus their attention on analyzing, evaluating, and reacting to what was said. One of the vital functions of listening is to provide the opportunity to empathize. People need to be listened to—carefully, critically, emotionally, and empathetically in order to enrich human relations and increase sensitivity.

The best way to be a better listener is to want to be a better listener. Do not place all the responsibility for communication on the speaker. Free yourself from distractions by the speaker's personal mannerisms, his voice, or an awkward arrangement of the room in which he speaks. Although the speaker should largely control these elements, should he not do so, a good listener makes every effort to compensate.

Nonverbal Signals

Good listening requires not only concentration on the meaning of the language but also a careful perception and evaluation of non-verbal signals

---

[2]R. G. Nichols and L. A. Stevens, *Are You Listening?* (New York: McGraw-Hill, 1957).
[3]O.M. Walter and R. L. Scott, *Thinking and Speaking* (New York: Macmillan, 1962), pp. 134–140.

conveyed by tonal quality, inflection, and intensity.[4] These vocal signals reflect inner feelings and perhaps unintended attitudes of the speaker. Although a well-modulated voice supported by diaphramatic breathing may be the result of good training, it is not a valid indicator of intelligence or human sensitivity. Sharp changes in pitch and intensity can, however, indicate an inner tension, aggressiveness, or disagreement. It is safe to generalize that a lower, more controlled pitch suggests relaxation and assuredness. A narrowed mouth and fixed facial features produce a rigid, monotonous articulation that frequently suggests defensiveness and anxiety. Anxiety and aggression are also communicated by excessive volume, rapid delivery, and the use of many words when a few would suffice.

A quiet voice that requires great energy from the audience simply to hear may indicate an individual with low self-esteem or, conversely, one who is so preoccupied with himself that he is unconcerned about the perceptions of his audience.[5]

Language Signals

Good listeners should also be aware of the vocabulary used by the speaker as signals for unintended attitudes.[6] Frequent use of "I" and "me" may indicate an individual who is egocentric, anxious, or perhaps even hostile to the audience. On the other hand, failure to ever use the personal pronoun may indicate an unwillingness to reveal one's inner feelings.

Unhappy, suspicious individuals tend to project these feelings through an excessive use of judgmental words. They frequently evaluate conditions, people, and situations as "horrendous," "superb," "terrific," "asinine," or "stupid." Nothing is ever neutral.

A fairly good indicator of the rigid and overly controlled individual is a low active vocabulary. This defensive, tense person tends to repeat the same words and phrases, almost to the point of patterning his expression. Conversely, openness and confidence are indicated by a greater variety in language choice.

We can tell a great deal about what the individual is thinking if we analyze his metaphors. When variety in metaphorical reference is evident in one's speech, this usually indicates a positive, thoughtful, creative mind. When metaphorical variety is heavily concentrated in one area, the listener may well look for significant meaning. Metaphor that refers to war or

[4]R. I. Johnson, M. Schalekamp, and L. A. Garrison, *Communication: Handling Ideas Effectively* (New York: McGraw-Hill, 1956), pp. 70–78.

[5]S. J. Baker, "The Theory of Silence," *Journal of General Psychology* 53 (1955), 145–167.

[6]J. R. Davitz, *The Communication of Emotional Meaning* (New York: McGraw-Hill, 1964).

fighting may reveal militant and aggressive feelings. Analogous reference to health, happiness, and the "wonders of nature" are usually associated with a positive, productive, and happy individual.[7]

Silence can also convey a variety of attitudes, including defiance, contemplativeness, grief, respect, or disinterest, and may serve to terminate the discussion.

Generalizing

The danger in placing too much significance in these vocal and vocabulary signals is the same danger inherent in any generalization—that of drawing hasty conclusions supported only by quick perception. Although vocal tone, quality, timber, and pitch, whether intentionally or unintentionally, may serve as valuable guides to enhancing meaning, they must never be considered as the principal or sole agent of communication. The listener should recognize these general communication qualities but keep a firm perspective about their importance when considering the speaker's intention and when evaluating the quality of presentation. Yes, good listening involves both the consideration of what is said and what is not, but the speaker must finally be held responsible only for his ideas delineated through language!

Emotional Response

Good listeners do not allow their emotional response toward ideas, people, groups, colors, style in clothing or unusual situations to influence their ability to listen accurately and to evaluate what has been said. Preconceived and fixed ideas are obvious barriers to listening, as they are to all other forms of communication. When we have preconceived notions, we immediately start forming a rebuttal to statements contrary to our own beliefs. While we are forming this defense of our own ideas, we are not listening to what the other individual has said. We are, rather, trying to frame questions which will embarrass or confuse the person who has now become our "adversary." Composing refutation and listening are not compatible activities. Hear the entire argument before you answer it.

The ability to hear an argument to its completion without interruption will permit a full comparison of our beliefs and those ideas with which we may not agree. The determination to be fair, to share, and to compare are habits of listening that help establish an environment in which comprehension, good will and compatibility may flourish.

[7]W. Pearce and R. Conklin, "Non-Verbal Vocalistic Communication and Perception of a Speaker," *Speech Monographs* 38 (1971), 235–241.

Reaction Time

Although a listener cannot make a detailed comparison, evaluation, or decision regarding the worth of what he hears while each word or sentence is being spoken, he does have more time than required to simply hear. People speak at a rate of 100–175 words per minute, but most individuals think much more rapidly. Reading comprehension tends to be between 350 and 500 words a minute.[8] If we use reading comprehension as a gauge for how fast we think, then an abundance of time is available for reflection as we listen. How wisely we use this time determines our efficiency as listeners. If we use it to daydream, to formulate negative opinions about the speaker and what he says, to prepare refutation for contentions he makes, or to make detailed notes of the text of his speech, we have wasted valuable time and have set up barriers to good listening.

CONTROL AND EVALUATION

A good listener must want to listen; he must concentrate his full energies on what is being said. He must try to control his environment, being comfortable but not so comfortable that relaxation causes collapse; he must maintain good muscle tone. He can control the temperature of the room, the lighting in the room, and he can place himself at an appropriate distance from the speaker in order to comprehend both the verbal and the nonverbal signals—but although he notices the nonverbal signals, he does not let them detract from what is being said with language. Listening requires an active analysis in search for the main ideas, the point of view, what is said, and what is implied. Astute listeners try to recognize the principal thesis and determine the main supporting evidence; they anticipate what is going to be said in the context of the conversation. They listen carefully to verify these predictions, and following a listening experience, they review to see if their anticipation or prediction is valid. They recognize the relationship of the supporting material to the main ideas and the amplification of the main ideas through example, analogy, statistics, or whatever else the speaker chooses. Careful review of the supporting material makes it easier to evaluate the quality of the ideas.

Note Taking

If you take notes, make them brief. Note taking should not be a complete chronicle of what was said but rather a simple reminder. When one becomes too involved in note taking, he loses the thread of the speaker's

[8] R. G. Nichols, "This Business of Listening," *American Trade Association Executive Journal V* (January 1956), 49–58.

thought, established through his transitions, and one may even lose a complete idea because he is so busy recording a previous and attractive point.

Selection

Listening is a selective and controlled process that allows us to decide what we should pay attention to and what we should disregard; obviously we cannot listen to everything within our range of hearing.

Listening is affected by previous experience. Should what we hear be irreconcilably different from our experience, we tend to stop listening. On the other hand, should what we hear be absolutely compatible with our past experience, we may also stop listening—because we feel that we already know the material. Both of these behavior patterns are the result of anticipation; we are reacting before the presentation of the material has been concluded. These practices must be discriminatingly employed, lest they become communication barriers.

A distinguished professor leading a seminar of twelve graduate students, of whom I was one, impressed all of us with his ability to grasp and state the essence of our discussion at the end of each seminar session. We attributed this ability to the professor's listening and note-taking skills because we observed him writing copious notes during the presentation of the student papers. One day, a graduate student "unintentionally" observed the professor's notes, which read as follows: "(1) Get milk and cottage cheese from grocery (2) Pick up Rose at 3:30 (3) Cocktails at 5:00—have both dry and regular Manhattans—get Angostura Bitters (4) Chuck does not like Martinis." My friend was not able to read the entire list; however, we concluded that the professor's skill in synthesizing did not depend on his full attention to what was being said. Unfortunately most individuals do not have the kind of mind that permits divergent activity coupled with full comprehension.

Anticipation

Too many people do not listen because they are planning what they are going to say when it is their turn to speak. Because the talker tends to dominate the communication situation, most people find it more enjoyable to talk than to listen. The talker feels that he or she is an important generator of ideas and therefore is in control of the situation.[9] I have sat in meetings where the agenda was poorly planned and where, as a result of a lack of direction, no one listened to anyone else because everyone was too concerned with formulating his own contribution when it was his turn to speak. Invariably people left the room saying, "What in the world was that

[9]W. A. Conboy, *Working Together . . . Communication in a Healthy Organization* (Columbus, Ohio: Charles E. Merrill, 1976), pp. 73–77.

meeting about?'' "I didn't get anything from that," "I didn't learn anything I didn't know before," "I've got better things to do," and "Why in the world did we meet?" These questions could be answered by a simple statement: "We didn't listen to each other, and therefore we left as uninformed as when we came."

MOTIVATE BY LISTENING

One of the best ways to influence the thought and action of another individual is not to talk to him or at him but to listen to him. When we find out what he believes and judge that it is acceptable or desirable, no further action is necessary. Should we judge that his thoughts and beliefs are unacceptable or counterproductive, then we have a clear foundation for planning and influencing change. When we have listened fully to another individual, the possibility of his reciprocating that courtesy is strong.

Don't just listen for facts—although facts are important. Listen for ideas, for concepts, feelings, and nuances that connote hidden points of view. Listen for inflection and other nonverbal communication. Listen empathically.

A Listening Profile

To develop good listening, be aware of the distractions in your own behavior that interfere with comprehension. A personal listening profile, which you draw, will do much to improve your awareness of listening barriers. To what things, to which people, and under what circumstances do you listen well? Do you listen for concepts or facts? Do you listen better to those in superior positions? What environmental conditions encourage your attention? What physical posture? What time of day?

Cultivate the attitude that no topic is uninteresting—that one may profit by carefully and analytically listening for the main ideas in any speech. Concentrate on the content and the message and not on the speaker's delivery. Don't be distracted or overstimulated by emotional reaction to ideas with which you disagree, or words, labels, or categories which may be offensive or repulsive. When you recognize that overstimulation can retard communication, anticipate your reaction to possible stimuli and effect a control mechanism which allows you to continue to listen for content. Don't listen to only that which is easy to understand. Developing the habit of concentrating specifically on difficult concepts will broaden one's perception and strengthen one's mind through this intellectual calesthenic.

Listening is a skill that can be developed slowly but firmly through practice that becomes habit.

OVERCOME BARRIERS CAUSED BY SEX, AGE, AND RACE

Chapter Four

BARRIERS CAUSED BY SEX

The primary barrier to productive communication between the sexes is attitude—attitude developed by a culture and socialization process that have arbitrarily assigned sex roles and demanded certain behavior as a result of this stereotyping.

Women compose about forty percent of the work force in the United States but occupy only about five percent of the managerial positions.[1] Recent state and federal legislation has made it possible for more women to compete for positions in middle-management situations in federal, state, and local government, and fair-employment practices require that women be given equal opportunity in businesses and industry; nevertheless, there remains a constant communication barrier between the sexes that prevents progress and productive cooperation.

Values

Many females are raised by their parents to be docile, self-depreciating, passive "helpmates" for their husbands; therefore, their choice of language and nonverbal behavior tends to manifest these traits.

[1]O. J. Harris, Jr., *Managing People at Work* (Santa Barbara, Calif.: John Wiley and Sons, 1976), p. 483.

Men, on the other hand, are trained to be aggressive, ambitious, and frequently proud. Language and nonverbal behavior growing from these traits are naturally different from those developed by a woman.[2]

Different communication patterns in men and women can also be attributed to the traditional division of labor among the sexes. Women are thought of primarily as homemakers, and when they do work, they find themselves in positions with little authority, requiring service and subservience to others. This affects their conversational patterns and nonverbal behavior. A man, on the other hand, uses more aggressive speech, hand gestures, and body movements partially as a result of his traditionally superior position in the work force.

The social conditions described produce different values among men and women. The male is more externally motivated and seeks evaluation, achievement, respect, and independence while the female values most highly identity with others, duty, loyalty, harmony, and family and home. Because of these values, the male places his interests and his achievements first and directs his full energies to achieving specifically defined goals. The female, being more responsive to the needs of others, usually assigns her interests a lower priority and gains her desires and recognition indirectly through the achievements of her husband and children.[3] Such divergent values and goals motivate different communication patterns.

Myths

Several unsupportable myths about women in the work force have also prevented their upward mobility. Among the most blatant are: (a) "Women are too emotional to make the rational decisions required of a manager." (b) "Women are sick or absent from work more often than men." (c) "Women do not have the drive to succeed because they do not need to work." (d) "Women have a higher turnover rate than men." (e) "Women do not have the capacity for scientific and technical skills."[4] These misconceptions can be put to rest by logic and a few facts.

In a study conducted by Reefe, Newstrom, and Monczka, female managers were found to be equal to men in the abilities of abstract thinking, communication skills, and objectivity. They were found to be superior in interacting with other individuals.[5] Other studies have shown that women are

[2]D. Jongeward and D. Scott, *Women As Winners* (Reading, Mass.: Addison-Wesley, 1976), pp. 4–16 and 63–77.

[3]*Ibid.*, pp. 272–275.

[4]L. C. Pogrebin, *Getting Yours: How to Make the System Work for the Working Woman* (New York: Avon Books, 1975), pp. 65–156.

[5]W. Reefe, J. W. Newstrom, and R. M. Monczka, "Exploding Some Myths About Women Managers," *California Management Review,* Summer 1975, p. 73.

more sensitive to the behavior and nuances of language than are men.[6] This can be a powerful advantage in communicating attentiveness and maintaining interaction with others.

The charge that women are too sensitive to make "hard decisions" can be answered by the fact that large corporations are spending thousands of dollars for "sensitivity training" for middle and top management personnel because they discovered that management's lack of humaneness in decision making and other interpersonal activities is a major cause of inefficiency. Therefore, some of the qualities women possess, which were previously assumed to be debilitating, are now being included regularly in management training of men. Awareness of feelings and adaptation to the impressions and actions they stimulate increases understanding and lifts morale.[7]

Women have also been victimized by the myths associated with genetic difference. In the past it has been supposed, and many people still believe, that raging monthly hormonal imbalance plagues women, making them prey to their emotions and thus unstable and unfit for positions of responsibility. However, scientists are discovering that men as well as women have monthly cycles of physical, emotional, and intellectual highs and lows that are biologically determined. Furthermore, men as well as women go through menopausal periods during which hormonal adjustments take place.[8] Both men and women can appropriately control their highs and lows to prevent these periods from interfering with performance of their daily tasks. Many women have unfortunately been taught by their mothers that they will "feel bad" at certain times each month; these mothers have provided models of behavior that young women continue to emulate. Knowing that both men and women have periods of discomfort caused by recurring biological and chemical changes should help dispel the myth that women in particular are incapable of ongoing responsibility.

An unhurried look at the 1976–77 figures compiled by the United States Bureau of Labor Statistics reveals that men tend to take longer and more frequent sick leave than women. The same report also indicates that the turnover rate for women is only slightly higher than for men.[9]

In answer to the charge that women lack proper motivation to suc-

[6]B. W. Eakins and R. G. Eakins, *Sex Differences in Human Communication* (Boston: Houghton Mifflin, 1968), pp. 14–21 and 72–73.

[7]E. D. Koontz, *Views of Women Achievers* (New York: Management-McKay and Associates, 1977), pp. 68–69.

[8]S. Fogg, "The Ups and Downs of Human Behavior Cycles," *Chicago Daily News,* April 20, 1973, p. 23.

[9]M. G. Burrow, *Women: A Worldwide View of Their Management Development Needs* (New York: AMACOM [A Division of the American Management Association] 1976), p. 6.

ceed, one need only observe the strengths and activities of the many professional women's associations such as the Coalition of Labor Union Women, International Business and Professional Women, and Associated Country Women of the World, which have strongly articulated and clearly defined women's increasing desire to succeed in managerial positions. The astonishing number of widowed and divorced women in today's labor force making less than $10,000 in annual salary argues strongly for both the need and desire for upward mobility. A woman's motivation can be as compelling as a man's.[10]

In science and technology, women have so fully and admirably demonstrated their ability in recent years that only complete ignorance of the facts would cause one to have any doubt about their competency.[11]

Attitudes

In answer to the contention that both men and women prefer to be supervised by a man, Crawley, Leviton, and Quinn compiled statistics from hundreds of individuals and scores of organizations that indicate that there is no appreciable difference in attitude or performance by men or women who have *actually* worked under a female supervisor.[12]

An old sexism was founded upon the belief that men were much more skillful and competent as managers than were women. A new sexism or antifeminism seems to be based on the belief that women are as competent and skilled as men; therefore, men fear the competition.

There is more than one way to perform a managerial job, so we should not make sexist comparisons about style. Women can determine their own leadership patterns, ones which suit their personalities and strengths. A manager's skill should be judged upon results and not upon the personality of the manager.[13]

Part of the problem of male/female communication is that women are commonly thought to have lost something when they become successful, while men are almost inevitably assumed to have gained in stature. Unfortunately women often have to sacrifice something—perhaps family, marriage, or noncompetitive relationships with men—but certainly not their femininity to gain position and mobility. Too frequently our society attributes a woman's success to luck or legislation but assumes that men who succeed do so because they are capable. We attribute male failure to bad

[10]P. J. Gordon, "Management Research and Reality," *The Conference Board Record,* October 1974, p. 51.

[11]*Ibid.*

[12]J. E. Crawley, T. E. Leviton, and R. P. Quinn, "Facts and Fiction About the American Working Woman," *I. S. R. Newsletter* (publ. by Institute for Social Research, University of Michigan) vol. 1, no. 16, October 1972, p. 45.

[13]D. C. Basil, *Women in Management* (Cambridge, Mass.: Harvard University Press, 1972), pp. 95–99.

luck and female failure to inadequacy. A desire for success in both men and women derives from the same drive to acquire fame, money, power, and security, and the strategies for achieving these do not differ; therefore, pejorative comparisons of the sexes are unwarranted and unjustified.

Strong-willed women who are articulate in expressing their desires may be considered by both men and women as "bitchy" or "butchy." On the other hand, a man with this ability is "sure" and "firm." What really matters is not the assessment of vigor and authority but the results that the male or female manager is able to achieve through his or her behavior. A woman need not conceal or restrain her competitiveness any more than a man. A female manager cannot be assertive simply by using charm; she must use persuasion and tactful pressure supported by well-reasoned and well-prepared evidence.

Because people tend to assume that women are subordinates in most working situations, female managers must display a bearing and commanding voice that indicate to all those she deals with that she "means business." Although it is important, perhaps even necessary, to have friendly interactions in order to accomplish goals, any manager needs to know that she is there in order to accomplish a task and not necessarily to be liked by her colleagues or to like them.[14] Women expect, and are expected, to be competent within an organization; a good supervisor never expresses amazement when a female performs a job well; she must be recognized for the achievement, not because she was a woman who attained it.

Self-Image

Some female managers suffer from a poor self-image. One of the best ways to improve one's self-image is to do something for someone else. Frequently when a woman helps another person, she learns to enjoy that individual. The other person in turn is attracted by her sense of responsibility and responsiveness to his or her needs; this response enhances the manager's self-esteem. However, one cannot spend the entire day helping others. Managers must plan their daily schedule to insure time for full participation in long-range planning and to concentrate appropriate attention on issues of the day. Planning and evaluation provide the framework for goal accomplishment—the kind of achievement one can measure and take pride in accomplishing. Success elicits positive feedback, which results in increased self-assurance.

Any manager, male or female, can enhance his or her self-image by maintaining good health and physical appearance. Dress neatly and appropriately, and maintain proper hygiene and grooming. When one knows that he or she makes a good appearance, self-confidence is automatically increased, and a positive personality is projected, which in turn increases one's power of persuasion.

[14]Pogrebin, *op. cit.*, pp. 117–122.

Unhappiness and boredom also affect one's self-esteem and in turn one's ability to communicate with others. Indifference to others gradually promotes indifference to one's own welfare and results in a lack of enthusiasm and diminished performance. When unhappiness and boredom with a job are not reconcilable, one should leave the position and find another job with greater opportunity for contentment.

Language and Speech

Many communication barriers between men and women are caused by other commonly held beliefs or feelings that have become part of the lore of a sexist society. Women are believed by both men and women to talk more than do men. Women are further believed to talk about less serious matters than men, to use different language, and to digress frequently in their discourse. On the other hand, men are believed to adopt a language and style of discourse that is "directly to the point"—free of abstraction and elaboration.

Even if these beliefs were to be substantiated by research, the best styles of discourse used by *both* sexes should be incorporated by both. Men need to be better listeners, especially in male/female conversation, and women need to develop their skills in analysis and evaluation and the use of humor to reinforce an idea.

A woman's speech tends to be more involved with interpersonal relations; it is more indirect, more polite, more concerned with feelings than with facts. A man's speech tends to be more involved with external matters and factual or statistical material; as such, it is more direct and more assertive. Men tend to use more objective terms and phrases when they describe people, places, and things, while women tend to use more interpretive language. Women are much more conscious of the nuances of shade, form, and texture; men consider such details irrelevant or inconsequential. Women generally use fewer expletives because while men feel that these reinforce their power and strength, women feel that the use of such words is vulgar or masculine and therefore should be avoided.[15] Howard Rosenfeld in 1966 discovered that women are less likely to complete sentences than are men and that women tend to answer questions rather than ask them in male/female interaction.[16]

Still other communication barriers are caused by the stereotyping of language and meaning associated with sex. For example, a woman is thought to *chat* or *gossip* while a man is thought to *discuss* or *describe.* A woman is *picky* or *fussy* while a man is *careful* and *fastidious.* And a woman has *wrinkles* but a man has *character lines.* When a woman is forceful and insistent, she may be perceived

[15]H. Sachs, E. Schegloff, and G. Jefferson, "A Simplest Semantics for the Organization of Turn-Taking for Conversation," *Language* 50 (1974): pp. 696–735.

[16]H. M. Rosenfield, "Approval-Seeking and Approval-Inducing Functions of Verbal and Non-Verbal Responses in the Dyad," *Journal of Personality and Social Psychology* (1966): pp. 597–605.

as *hysterical;* a male behaving this way is *persistent.* Think for a moment about the different shades of meaning between the following words, which should possess the same values: *patron* and *matron, sir* and *madam, tailor* and *seamstress, master* and *mistress.* It has been an unequal world, and language is still used to maintain that inequality.[17] Terms peculiar to gender and their potentially denigrating associations need to be selectively used lest they promote or connote second-class status for more than half our population. Avoid evaluating objects and situations in terms of gender. Both sexes should avoid language that treats either sex as an object or in a dehumanizing manner. Describe individuals as people, citizens, inhabitants, workers, and supervisors, rather than use words that require *man* as a prefix or suffix.

Barbara and Gean Eakins believe that women need to eliminate a tendency to add questions to their assertions, such as "don't you think so," "do you agree," "didn't you," "isn't she," and "isn't it"—all of which indicate self-doubt and a hesitancy to express and support an opinion. Women should also avoid qualifiers and disclaimers; these invite disputation and suggest an unwillingness to accept responsibility for what is said. Avoid such expressions as "I could be wrong," "I'm not sure of this," "You may not agree, but . . .," "I suppose," "I guess," and "Maybe this is okay."[18]

Managers must learn to describe men and women in terms of their physical, social, and mental attributes, avoiding sexual innuendoes that suggest positive or negative qualities peculiar to either. Identify people in terms of their roles within the organization, not in terms of their sex or relationship to their spouse. When we stop using language that suggests a stereotyped expectation, attitudes and, therefore, behavior will be improved.

Because women are more firmly categorized regarding ability as a result of projected vocal quality than are men, women will profit significantly in male/female communication by conscious control of timing, force, pitch, timbre, and resonance, all of which can be used to suggest self-assurance and conviction. The importance of proper vocal development for the female manager is implicit in the premise that females frequently achieve their position and status by their *total projection of personality* and competence (voice included), while men receive their standing in the organization and in society by *what they do;* the position men hold is more important than who holds the position. Thus, status and achievement signaled by precision in speech appear to be more important for females than for males, at least for the present.

Communication barriers occur when men and women cannot readily adapt to each other's communication style. Women need to become less concerned with personal opinion, personality, and attitudes and more concerned with facts. This will prevent them from being generalized by men as being illogical. Conversely, men need to become more conscious of how human feelings can modify

[17]Eakins and Eakins, *op. cit.,* pp. 112–143.
[18]*Ibid.*

interpretation of factual situations. This will cause them to be perceived as more benevolent and humane.

Nonverbal Signals

In male/female communication women look more at the person with whom they are talking than do men. The more positive attitude the female has toward the person she is talking with, the more prolonged the eye contact. Women also turn away more readily after eye contact has been made—which, signals deference or submission.[19]

Women tend to keep their arms closer to their bodies and to gesture less; their gestures generally are more restrained and less expressive. Women also tend to sit straighter and more rigidly when talking; they lean less than males—either toward or away from the other person. Upright posture with knees pressed together or crossed tightly, one knee over the other, has been taught to women since childhood as the "ladylike" way to sit. Women do tend to display more gestures when conversing with a male than when conversing with another female.

J. L. Freedman discovered that women are approached more closely for conversation by both men and women than are men. This occurs (a) because a woman perceives her territorial space as being smaller than a man does his; (b) because she desires more intimate conversational relationships than a man; or (c) because she is more willing to be influenced by others. It may also mean that women are considered subordinate and not entitled to as much space as men.[20]

In conversation, males should generally avoid touching female coworkers because this may be interpreted as an assertion of authority. Males should also guard against thinking that a touch by a female worker is an improper overture. Male and female touching should have the same value and communicate the same meaning. A woman need not be reluctant to touch another woman or a man if the gesture is intended to reinforce a statement and not to communicate sexual interest. When a woman does not wish to be touched, she can terminate the touching by staring hard, directly into the other person's eyes or by simply moving away. She should never allow herself to be intimidated, dominated, or embarrassed by another person's unwanted touch.[21]

Men should concentrate on looking at a woman when she speaks; they should not interrupt or distract by making an unusual movement or noise. Men should actively reinforce a woman's communication with good eye contact, positive nonverbal body position and gesture, and occasional smiling and head nodding, and should respond when signaled to do so. Men need to learn to "take their turn" in male/female conversation. Being an active, not a dominant, participant will insure a smooth flow and exchange of information.

[19]*Ibid.,* p. 150.
[20]J. L. Freedman, "The Crowd: Maybe Not So Maddening After All," *Psychology Today* 4 (1971): p. 59.
[21]Eakins and Eakins, *op. cit.,* pp. 172–177.

Women tend to smile more than men. Since infancy, women have been taught to smile in order to avoid criticism or punishment. This submissive nonverbal behavior should be controlled because it weakens a woman's position in male/female discourse. Women also tend to drop their eyes or look away when confronted with an unpleasant situation. This defensive behavior also weakens one's position. Look the other person directly in the eye when it is appropriate to do so; eye contact reinforces one's strength and the control necessary for rebuttal. During a confrontation, don't tilt the head to one side; this softens your directness and implies submissiveness.

Assertion Not Aggression

Judi Brownell, of the Communications Department of the State University of New York at Cortland, believes that women are frequently confronted with sexist remarks and "put downs." Brownell advises them not to laugh off such remarks or smile away their discomfort. For many women, a smile is like a reflex action in embarrassing or anger-provoking situations. Brownell advises women to take time to respond in their own way and not to feel pressured to react emotionally. If the woman does not smile in appreciation, the man will get the message that his remark was not funny. She may wish to say simply, "I don't think that was funny!" If the man responds, "What's the matter, doll, no sense of humor?" a woman may repeat her initial comment without getting into a prolonged discussion or defense of her reaction.[22]

A few other stock responses that can be used are: "That remark is demeaning," "That comment is really in poor taste," "You must be kidding!" "You can't be serious!" and "You must feel threatened or uptight about this situation." Avoid name-calling or prolonged responses that can be interpreted as aggressive unless you intend to terminate a relationship. When a man uses obscene language in the presence of a woman, she may choose to answer him with even more shocking terms. This technique may embarrass the man and cause him to modify his behavior. The woman, however, runs the risk of being considered foul-mouthed or vulgar, so she had better be selective in using this verbal mirror technique. The more often a woman effectively handles negative reactions from others, the less frequently such responses will be necessary.

Choose firmness rather than hostility in correcting unacceptable behavior; focus on issues rather than personalities; have a ready response to offensive remarks and categorize such remarks as being generally offensive

[22]J. Brownell, Unpublished paper delivered at Assertion Workshop, Cortland, N.Y., 1977.

to *people*, not just to men or to women. These are the best ways to combat sexist conditioning.[23]

A good female manager must learn the distinction between assertiveness and aggressiveness. The latter is hostile; it attacks the individual and not the problem. Assertion presents you and your ideas; aggression attacks another person, sometimes with the intent to destroy. Aggression is usually counterproductive because it does not elicit desired and lasting change; it establishes new communication barriers.

Confrontation

A woman can avoid certain confrontations and the ensuing communication barriers by thoughtful anticipation. For example, my daughter-in-law, an attractive lawyer living in a large eastern city, told me that she frequently had difficulty paying for a business lunch, especially if the client was male. Although she had an expense account, the male accompanying her invariably insisted on paying the check. A man may think that this is expected, appropriate, and gentlemanly for him to pay, but if he has many luncheon engagements with a female lawyer, he may come to resent the fact that, even though they have a business arrangement, he always "picks up the tab."

I advised my daughter-in-law that when she makes a reservation for a business luncheon, she should provide her credit card number and request that the check be charged to her account. If this arrangement is not possible, she should instruct the maitre d', when she enters the restaurant, that the check should be delivered to the cash register; she can then pay for it on leaving. If the check never comes to the table, there will be no discussion about who is to pay—and therefore no confrontation. A woman can thus prevent possible resentment when one of her equals is forced constantly to bear the financial burden of their relationship. I also advised my daughter-in-law that upon entering a taxi with a male client, she immediately tell the driver that she intends to pay the fare. This preplanning and assertion will gain respect and minimize any resentment or any implied expectation or threat about a man's responsibility in a male/female business and quasi-social relationship.

My daughter-in-law has advised me that application of the above suggestions has proven very valuable in improving her interpersonal relations with male clients.

[23]M. V. Higginson and T. L. Quick, *The Ambitious Woman's Guide to a Successful Career* (New York: AMACOM [A Division of the American Management Association] 1975), pp. 147-149.

Sexism

For a woman to achieve competence and recognition, she must overcome sexist-motivated prejudices. Sexism flourishes when both men and women fail to realize that pejorative comparisons are made because they have been conditioned all their lives to behave in a sexist way. These prejudices are reinforced in organizations where women are treated as less competent than men, thought of as sex objects, highly regarded for their anatomical virtues, referred to as "the girls," and consistently relegated to insignificant or subordinate roles when ideas are discussed and responsibility assigned.

To insure dignity and equality for women, we must stop laughing at jokes that demean women and refuse to tolerate chauvinistic behavior. As long as women continue to suffer from stereotyped expectations, both men and women are prevented from developing constructive methods of working together, and the organization loses an important ingredient in cooperation. When you hear sexist comments about men or women, ask why the speaker reached that conclusion. Often when a person has to justify his or her prejudices rationally, the person's bias becomes obvious to him or her and is then modified or eliminated.

Women should resent sexist attitudes in their organizational interactions; however, they should resist the impulse to give vent immediately to their resentment through angry outbursts; they should not flaunt their activities in "women's lib" groups or make a daily issue of women's rights. They simply must require equal pay, equal consideration, and equal protection commensurate with their qualifications and productivity. Women must avoid stereotyped behavior and develop self-confidence and a flexible style that emphasizes their particular strengths. They must never demean themselves, never let anyone else demean them, and never demean another female colleague in public; "to do so is to accept the judgment that a woman is inferior."[24] Both sexes must continue to develop skills and attitudes which promote male/female communication.

A woman need not lose her femininity in order to be spirited, accomplished, and fulfilled; she just has to create the correct impression of authoritative competence. As more and more women of every age enter the job market, male and female work patterns are becoming increasingly similar.

BARRIERS CAUSED BY AGE

A serious communication barrier in many organizations is caused by age differential in the working force. This is an especially difficult problem for

[24]E. Shanahan, *Views from Women Achievers* (New York: Management—McKay and Associates, 1977), p. 105.

a young manager who inherits a staff of subordinates who have been with the organization for ten, perhaps even twenty years, prior to his affiliation.

Attitudes and Values

The conflict of youth and age is not a new one, but it has been intensified and compounded by the much publicized discontent of youth in the 1960's and early 1970's. In 1968, Henry Winthrop noted, "The older generation-industrial man lives by the values of the system of free enterprise: success, comfort, security, status-striving, competition, power, money, . . . the quest for distinction. The younger generation, post-industrial man, believes in establishing a personal identity, authentic relations between man and man, more decentralization, politically . . . socially . . . and the exploitation of science, technology, and affluence to improve the conditions of man rather than for a profit, . . ."[25]

Whether Winthrop's generalization is correct or not, many members of the older generation feel alienated from youth. When a young manager assumes supervisory authority over older people, any incompatibility, if left untreated, can seriously impair organizational goals and operation.

Regardless of the age of his subordinates, an efficient manager makes every effort to resolve strife and jealousy, and to recognize individuals' specific needs, desires, and perceptions in the context of their background, work experience, outside responsibilities, education, goals and how well they have satisfied those goals within the organization.[26]

Many older workers have less education than younger ones; the former are naturally fearful and sometimes jealous of these "come-lately-over-educated-smart alecks." To keep the older worker productive and secure, an effort must be made to involve older and younger workers in cooperative tasks so that the experience of one and the energy and education of the other merge to attain a common goal. Ancillary values of this cooperation may indeed be a greater understanding of the values, needs, and capabilities of both participants. When understanding is present, attitudinal change is possible and worker compatibility and productivity will improve.

Dead Wood

In his book *Managerial Situations and How to Handle Them,* William Wachs points to specific problems in organizations caused by age and longevity.[27]

[25]H. Winthrop, "The Alienation of Post-Industrial Man," *Midwest Quarterly,* vol. 9, no. 2 (January 1968), p. 123.

[26]Harris, *op. cit.,* pp. 179–182.

[27]W. Wachs, *Managerial Situations and How to Handle Them* (West Nyack, N.Y.: Parker, 1977), p. 231.

First is the problem of "dead wood": a young manager encounters an organizational veteran who resists every suggested change and who, when he discovers that change is inevitable, refuses to participate. Instead, the veteran walks the halls, visits old friends, and does recreational reading at his desk. He completes reports only when they are demanded—usually late. He demonstrates no initiative, takes long coffee breaks, and is frequently absent because of "illness."

Two solutions are possible. First, the manager can urge early retirement; if that fails, he can exert such unpleasant pressure that the veteran will either do a better job or accept an opportunity to transfer to another unit. A manager's second option is to change the job of the older individual, making it seem like a promotion and appealing to his pride and experience as incentives for more productive behavior. The manager should also inform the veteran that this is a second but final opportunity to demonstrate his competence and cooperation and that should he fail in this new position, termination is certainly an alternative.

The best solution to "dead wood" is to prevent it; however, this is not possible when a manager inherits a nonproductive employee. Whatever the solution, the most important conclusion is that the unproductive employee must be removed quickly from a position that allows him to hinder the progress and productivity of others. Choose the most humane solution possible, but choose a solution consistent with the goals of the organization and these certainly include economic and efficient production.

Resistance to New People

The resistance-to-new-people syndrome is a problem frequently encountered by a new manager.[28] The recalcitrant employee reacts to the new manager and his ideas by advising fellow workers against cooperation, refusing to supply answers, giving misleading or inaccurate information, talking behind the manager's back, or even making sarcastic or snide and critical remarks in meetings about the manager's competence. He constantly reminds everyone, "This is not the way we used to do it."

To break down this communication barrier and to minimize counterproductive behavior, the new manager can do several things. He may embarrass the "resister" in front of his colleagues by asking him to substantiate his charges of incompetence; when the resister is unable to support his contentions, he may cease his disruptive behavior. At least his coworkers will recognize that he is primarily resisting a new supervisor. A second, softer, approach is to appeal to the resister's pride in his past achievements and to indicate the importance of his cooperation with the new manager in order to reach objectives. A new manager should explain to the person caus-

[28]M. R. F. Maier, *Playing Technique* (La Jolla, Calif.: University Associates, 1975), pp. 63–74.

ing difficulty how important he is to the total team effort, that his expertise and advice are greatly needed.

If these approaches do not work, the new manager must address the situation firmly and directly by pointing out that he considers continued resistance to be opposition to both the manager and the organization, that resistance is discrediting the dissident in the eyes of others, and that continued overt opposition will not be permitted. A new manager cannot allow prolonged resistance even if it means terminating an employee who has served with the company for years. Recognize the cause of resistance; try various tactics for overcoming resistance; insist upon a change of attitude and behavior that results in cooperation; or terminate the opposition.

Jealousy

A new manager may encounter jealousy and resentment among veterans who have been bypassed for the position he now fills. In this situation, the new manager must use persuasion to convince the veterans of their worth and importance to the organization, how he needs them to accomplish tasks, and how he values their loyalty and assistance. Seek the veterans' opinions; give them special consideration; appeal to the strength of each one—incorporating their ideas with your own so that solutions and actions that result from this cooperation seem to them a joint achievement. With time and skill on your part, *they* may even take pride in what *you* accomplish, say things like, "Taught the lad how to solve that problem," "He really wanted to know what I thought," "That boy's o.k.!" and "He's a fine fellow!" When the older worker comes to admire and respect his manager, his own self-esteem increases and so do his value and productivity.

Lost Ambition

Occasionally a new manager may encounter an employee who has lost his ambition, one who is completely satisfied with the position he has held for several years. He resists new responsibilities, opportunities for promotion, and change in routine. This person is satisfied to do only what he has been doing until he reaches the age of retirement. He simply does not want to "rock the boat" if it disturbs his schedule.

The manager has a choice of ignoring this individual's lethargy—so long as he does his job adequately. The manager should, however, inform the individual that he has no chance for promotion or salary increases and that subordinates who serve under him may move around and beyond him up the organizational ladder. Should the individual be satisfied with these conditions, the manager can be reasonably sure that he has a docile employee who will contribute at best only adequately to the organization.[29]

[29]*Ibid.*

However, should the manager recognize in this individual the necessity and potential for greater achievement, he might consider moving him to another position in hope that a new environment, new challenge, and new colleagues may motivate him to greater productivity. When a manager concludes that an individual's lack of ambition is interfering with the productivity of the organizational unit and the welfare of subordinates and colleagues, he must weigh the value of having a contented worker remain in a job he clearly prefers and handles adequately against replacing him with new, more dynamic, more ambitious potential leadership.

BARRIERS CAUSED BY RACE

Racial differences often affect our reactions and impair communication. Because of our cultural inheritance, we must make an active, constant effort to overcome ingrained prejudice and attitudes if we are to be more efficient managers dealing with all races.

Racism

Although education, experience, and an atmosphere of greater tolerance have reduced prejudice about sex, age, and religion, race remains almost as high a barrier as ever to full understanding among people. We have been taught to attach extraordinary significance to obvious differences in skin pigmentation. Our pattern of behavior regarding other races is based primarily on what other people have told us, what we have read, and what we assume, rather than on actual interracial experience. People have been taught to trust only their own race; that they can't really have a close relationship with someone of another race; that whites are trying to take advantage of blacks; that blacks and Chicanos are shiftless and uninformed; that whites are devious and possess undeserved power that they won't share with minorities; that Chicanos are in this country illegally and therefore should not have all the benefits that the system provides; that any minority person could really achieve if he tried; that minority men and women want to date and marry people of the majority race in order to "improve their situation"; that all native Americans are drunkards; that blacks are oversexed; that Puerto Ricans have come to New York City and Chicanos to California only for welfare benefits; and a variety of other prejudicial attitudes.

White people, black people, yellow people, and brown people in America have magnified their racial differences and have allowed them to become communication barriers. These barriers among the races will not be overcome unless all races recognize their responsibility in the communication process.

An Ethnic Perspective

Communication involves a transfer of meaning in terms we understand, expect, and empathize with, and this meaning is based largely on our own experience and culture. Herein lies the principal barrier to interracial communications. That each race has maintained its own culture, sometimes its own language, and certainly many of its own behavior patterns prevents an easy and appropriate exhange of feeling among the races. Each race tends to approach the communication situation from its own ethnic perspective. As individuals, we tend to accept our own beliefs and values without question, but we also fail to recognize how our views and values differ from those of a member of a different race.[30] In the United States, we have many cross-cultural and common values regardless of race, color, or creed. However, we magnify our differences, and it is these that are important and must be understood by each racial group if clear communication is to ensue. Racism is not simply discrimination in hiring and in opportunity, or an exercise in intolerance; it is these plus an irrational, negative feeling about those individuals different from ourselves.[31]

"Gaming" and Power

Power is a second deterrent to good interracial communication.[32] When one race, through its behavior, attempts to dominate another, conflict arises. The black, brown, or yellow person—being in the minority in the United States—may express his lack of power through disruptive actions or inattention. The minority person may "signify,"[33] by a variety of behavior patterns, that he does not agree with the system imposed upon him by the majority. Often one's color is used as a screen through which all communication is filtered.

Such strategies as beginning a conversation with "I don't expect to get a fair deal from you because I am black and you are white," obviously do not promote clear understanding. It is, nevertheless, a power strategy that puts the majority representative on the defensive and shifts the focus to complexion and away from the real point of discussion. Racial differences should never be used as a power factor or threat in the communication process.

[30]J. A. Blubaugh and D. L. Pennington, *Crossing Difference . . .*, (Columbus, Ohio: Charles E. Merrill, 1976), pp. 3–20.

[31]*Webster's Third International Dictionary.*

[32]W. D. Jacobson, *Power and Interpersonal Relations* (Belmont, Calif.: Wadsworth, 1972), pp. 5–9.

[33]The term "signify" is often used by blacks to describe an intentional ritualistic behavior which is insulting, demeaning, or degrading to others. "The dozens" and "sounding" are words also used to indicate the same verbal and nonverbal interaction. See W. Labov, "Rules for Ritual Insults," in *Rappin' and Stylin' Out,* ed. Thomas Kochman (Urbana: University of Illinois Press, 1972), pp. 265–314.

Reverse Discrimination

Some white people in America feel that the recent emphasis on equal employment is going to permit minorities less qualified than themselves to take their jobs. This, of course, is contrary to the intent of the legislation. Nevertheless, when whites behave defensively toward minorities, clear communication is invariably clouded, and the suspected potential power of minorities becomes a communication barrier. A clear explanation by management of the necessary reasons for hiring minorities will help to assure the majority that future competition for positions and promotions must and will be based upon qualifications and skill alone but will include all eligible people.

The matter of reverse discrimination in employment can be ethically and efficiently approached when parameters included in the job description clearly delineate minimum qualifications necessary for success in that position. When the parameters are extended to include a pool of all qualified applicants, the question is then asked, "What are the basic minimum qualifications that an individual needs to possess in order to be successful in this position?" The employer, rather than starting from the top test score, or other measurable criteria, and moving downward as he considers candidates, is able to look at the total applicant pool in order to make a selection that will insure appropriate representatives from minority and female applicants.

The problem of reverse discrimination is a serious one that must be dealt with directly by management. The fact that minority groups have long been denied equal opportunity for jobs for which they are qualified must be explained, and the fact that a minority person, with qualifications equal to those of a white person, must be given an opportunity to serve in order to make up for his lack of opportunity in the past will, in the long run, prove beneficial to the total organization by broadening the cultural and social opportunities to associate with all people who make up American society. If we truly believe in the tenets of the Constitution and the Bill of Rights, we cannot deny a qualified person, because of race, creed, or national origin, an opportunity to fill a job; indeed, we must welcome this individual into our midst with a teaching-and-learning, cooperative attitude. Only when each person is given the opportunity to fill the best job for which he is qualified will all people in America have the opportunity to realize all they are capable of being.

Myths

The myth of athletic and physical superiority of one race over another, and the conflicts that these false perceptions of power present, sometimes form lasting barriers to appropriate interaction with members of another race. When one race mimics the language, dress, behavior patterns, or hair style of another as a signal of acceptance, or a desire to communicate, these superficial signals often have the opposite effect of communicating a lack of sympathy, empathy, and real sincerity.[34] Such behavior and signaling are forms of deferring to the power—real or imagined—of another racial group or individuals within that group; they do not advance interpersonal relationships or solidify the communication process.

Good interracial communication overcomes differences, even though these differences are recognized, and allows each individual an equal opportunity to influence conclusions arrived at as a result of discussion.

Other Assumptions

In addition to the many racial assumptions that block communication and understanding (such as those held by black Americans that whites are materialistic, insincere, and power-hungry and those held by white Americans that blacks are superstitious, musical, and athletic and that Mexicans and Puerto Ricans are emotional, argumentative, and talkative) other, more subtle, assumptions are made.

To assume that color is unimportant in interpersonal relations; that all blacks, Mexicans, or other minority groups can be stereotyped in terms of their actions and reactions; that all minorities would welcome inclusion in "our white, superior society"; that, regardless of the evidence, we are free of racism, and that therefore we have a right to *help*—which really means control—minority people, is to perpetuate the very racism that we hope to overcome.[35] To assume that open recognition of color is going to embarrass someone whose complexion is different from one's own is to ignore the cultural value one places upon his own heritage and is a strong signal of feelings of racial superiority.

When white people assume that blacks are "too sensitive" and tend to overreact to real or imagined slurs, they should recall that blacks in the United States have been objects of discrimination, injustice, and a lack of opportunity for more than a hundred years, and from 1619 to 1862 they were legally in bondage, residents of this country by no choice of their own. The white majority in America must, therefore, "take the extra step" toward improving interracial communication.

We develop our racial assumptions from our background and experience; from what we hear, what we see; from our exposure to relatives, friends, and the institutions in which we participate. What we expect other

[34]W. D. Jacobson, *Power and Interpersonal Relations* (Belmont, Calif.: Wadsworth, 1972), pp. 54–82.

[35]B. M. Lee and W. H. Schmidt, "Toward More Authentic Relations Between Blacks and Whites," *Human Relations Training News* 13 (1969): 4–5.

people to be and do often is realized in their behavior. To overcome prejudiced points of view that block communication, we must look at the real value of the individual and somehow divorce ourselves from the attitudes and behavior we have been taught to expect from members of a group other than our own.

LANGUAGE BARRIERS

Several years ago a college "school of practice" bussed a group of minority students from a nearby urban center and enrolled them in the summer session with "regular" students. One morning, when the first-grade class was preparing for an art lesson, one of the visiting six-year-olds blurted out, "Teacher, I ain't got no paint and no brush!" A white student, son of a professor at the college, leaned over to the first lad and advised him, "You should say, I haven't any paint or brush," to which the first boy replied, "Go f--- yourself!"

The professor's son, in offering a correction, assumed that he was being helpful and that he was advancing communication. But everyone in the room understood what the visiting child needed, so communication was not advanced; as a matter of fact, just the opposite ensued, if we can judge by the hostility expressed in the minority child's response. If such hostility is evoked in a child, think how a demand for standard English blocks communication in adult conversation.

In interracial communication, one should not demand standard English, nor should one signal in any way that the grammar or syntax is incorrect. The principal requirement for language is understanding, and in order to have understanding, we must have some common knowledge of the meaning of the language used. When we do not understand the symbols used by another individual, then communication is marred. Occasionally, regional dialects and foreign accents impede communication, but usually language bariers result from extralinguistic symbols employed by different races, peculiar to the culture of each racial group.[36]

A lack of common symbols between the races is usually not the principal barrier to understanding; the larger barrier is rather our intolerance of language that does not meet our own rigid standards of semantics. A communicator who uses words peculiar in meaning to his racial group occasionally is trying to conceal or "put down" the individual with whom he is talking. If someone says, "That's heavy," or "You're bad," and he means, "That's an excellent idea worthy of considerable thought," and "You are

[36]J. F. Buck, "The Effects of Negro and White Dialectual Variations Upon Attitudes," *Speech Monographs* 35 (1968): 181–186.

good or thoughtful,'' or a "nice person,'' then obviously there is a divergence of definition that may interfere with communication.

Often language, especially that chosen by a young minority person, is peculiar to an inner-city group; such expressions as "crib,'' "duce n'a quarter,'' "du waz,'' and "ace-boon-coon,'' need to be accepted by management because they are used in the context of the individual's cultural environment and have a perfectly clear meaning to the person who uses them. When an executive does not respond appropriately to this langauge, he will not be able to communicate, and indeed he may feel that the minority individual talking with him does not wish to communicate. This may, of course, be a complete misunderstanding. "Hip talk'' should be avoided, but when used, it must be understood by both the speaker and the listener.

Syntax

Some white managers feel that blacks do not "talk their language'' and demand that they use standard English in order in communicate. If the meaning of a sentence is clear, accept that meaning and go on with the conversation. To make a correction during an interview or meeting is to comment negatively on the individual with whom you are talking. If you don't understand the language being used, it would be wise to say, "I'm not familiar with that term. Would you define what you mean so as to enlighten me? You and I have to work together, and we have to understand one another.'' To allow communication to be obscured by a lack of understanding of words is a practice management cannot afford.

Having said this, I do, however, firmly believe that words and phrases with no meaning outside a specific group should be avoided in interracial communication. Language that is used to disguise feelings and meaning subverts communication, in which the intention should be to share experiences and in interracial communication to share experiences among the races. Although language choice and meaning that are peculiar to members of one group may have a unifying purpose, they also have a way of excluding others. Language that does not rely upon common experience for definition is language that is ill-chosen and discourages further communication.

Words and Emotions

In interracial communication, one must be careful with language to assure its commonality of meaning, and one must also avoid words and phrases that automatically provoke an emotional response.[37] In a conversation with a friend who happens to be black, I used the word "spook." My intended meaning was that the person referred to as a "spook" had hung like a specter over the shoulder of another individual—had literally haunted that individual. My friend paused, looked at me, studied my face, and gave me some nonverbal signals that his meaning of "spook" was not the same as mine, and for a moment, our conversation—that is, our communication—was shattered by my thoughtless choice of language. I had forgotten all the negative and chilling connotations this term has for a black. How the robed Klan intimidated blacks and how whites had borrowed the term to describe a black who is confronted with danger.

"*You people,*" "when *you people* are ready for responsibility, you will get it," "I can't understand why *you people* are so upset," and "*you people* must help yourselves," are phrases that lump groups and suggest expected group behavior and reaction. Their use is detrimental to individual understanding and clearly signals a recognition or feeling of separation. Also, such phrases as "right on," "what's happenin'," "dig it," and "brother," when uttered by a white to a black denote a lack of sincerity. It is wise to avoid any flippant racial remark or phrase unless one is absolutely sure of the listener's attitudes and awareness. Even then, seemingly innocent overtures toward fellowship may be misinterpreted and fan smoldering coals of forgotten resentment.

Italians do not like to be called "paisano" by non-Italians, nor do Chicanos like to be called "amigo" by "Anglos," nor do Indians like to be called "chief" by anybody other than members of the tribe of which they may be chief. A white person, if he knows the meaning, certainly doesn't want to be called "Charlie" or "Mr. Charlie" by a black person. Such forms of address, even uttered in a spirit of good will, are insulting and should be deleted from one's vocabulary.

While speaking of deletions, I strongly urge that one avoid derogatory statements regarding women of an ethnic group other than one's own. All races tend to be sensitive and protective in this matter, and many men feel a personal threat and potential loss, perhaps even an assault on their own manhood when confronted with slurs about women of their race made by "outsiders."

Clear definitions are a keystone to understanding, and our definition of and use of words must constantly be expanded to accommodate new and different perspectives and perceptions. Developing a sensitivity to the connotations and denotations in language peculiar to a certain race is a first

[37]A. L. Rich, "Some Problems in Interracial Communication: An Interracial Group Case Study," *Central States Speech Journal* 22 (Winter 1971): pp. 228-235.

step toward promoting better understanding. Although sensitivity alone does not insure clarity, it certainly is a major step toward opening new channels of communication.

NONVERBAL BARRIERS

The significance of nonverbal behavior lies in the observer, not in the signaler. The receiver assigns meaning to behavior based upon his perceptions and experience; therefore, two receivers may interpret nonverbal signals in entirely different ways.[38] Nonverbal signaling between the races must be carefully interpreted so as not to provide unnecessary barriers to appropriate interaction across racial lines.

Complexion

In America, the most obvious nonverbal barrier is complexion. This nonverbal communication is critical when it prevents people of opposite races from advancing beyond the emotional and intellectual connotations that skin color produces. When we permit complexion to trigger a variety of prejudices about races different from our own, then, of course, we will never respond to a person individually. This kind of generalization becomes a serious barrier through which all future communication is filtered. Preconceived attitudes and judgment based upon race can be avoided if the differences in the races are noted and assigned positive rather than negative values.

Touch

A further deterrent to good interracial communication is our reluctance to touch someone of another race. Touching is more telling than other nonverbal communication because it requires an overt action and causes a physical sensation in ourselves and in the person whom we touch. In America, touching is generally reserved for people with intimate relationships or for close friends or relations, and it is sometimes used as a nonverbal signal of domination.[39] Touching a person of a different race can become a meaningful communicative symbol that has a positive effect on further communication.

[38]N. L. Knapp, *Non-Verbal Communication in Human Interaction* (New York: Holt, Rinehart and Winston, 1972), pp. 21–25.
[39]"A Picture of Power—No Bigger than a Man's Hand," *Psychology Today,* January 1972, p. 26.

Eye Contact

A little known nonverbal technique of communication used by blacks to express displeasure with whites is called "wallin'," or "eye balling."[40] This is accomplished by rolling the pupils of the eyes back toward the corners of the iris. If eye contact is avoided between the two individuals, the initiator of the eye-rolling has the satisfaction of having reacted in a negative way—even though direct confrontation does not occur. Eye behavior among the races that causes feelings of anxiety, doubt, and mistrust—whether intentional or unintentional, obvious or concealed—should be avoided.

Time

Promptness is also a problem in communication between races because different races place different values on the use of time. Traditionally, the white Protestant ethic has highly valued promptness and conservation of time. The black American and the Mexican American have not placed great value on keeping a tight time schedule,[41] preferring a more relaxed atmosphere in which everyone gets to express an opinion or debate the issues. Occasionally the failure to observe appointment times or meeting times is interpreted by whites as a minority protest against the system, and indeed promptness is selectively used for this purpose. Who waits for whom and for how long says important things about relationships. Failure to be prompt exerts a certain amount of control over the person kept waiting. Respect is shown by being early or on time and by accomplishing the business in as little time as is necessary. Of course, one shows respect for another by not only being on time but by leaving when the business has been completed. Time can be manipulated to communicate powerful positive or negative feelings among the races; it is a factor that must be considered and consciously controlled.

Space

We have recognized the necessity for possession of psychological and personal space. Violation of our space by someone of another race may be interpreted as an invasion that must be met with hostility.[42] It is natural to

---

[40]This behavior was demonstrated and its meaning described to the author by a black woman in southern Illinois when he was twelve years old. Also see B. G. Cooke, "Non-Verbal Communication Among Afro-Americans: An Initial Classification," in *Rappin' and Stylin' Out,* ed. Thomas Kochman, pp. 51–52.

[41]J. Horton, "Time and Cool People," in *Rappin' and Stylin' Out,* ed. Thomas Kochman, pp. 19–31.

[42]J. R. Gibb, "Defensive Communication," *The Journal of Communication* 11:3 (September 1961), pp. 140–143.

maintain and protect the space we have staked out around us, but we somehow feel more threatened when someone of another race advances on that space than we do if someone of our own race infringes. We will overcome tensions if we recognize and modify the powerful nonverbal signals we may be giving to someone of a different race who enters "our space." The significance of "racial" space or any other illogical attitudes and behaviors that separate rather than unify the races is based on a cultural environment in America that assigns divergent values to the races.

Conversation

There seem to be subtle but very clear differences in eye contact, body positioning, and spatial requirements between black and white communicants. Whites, when talking, tend to look away from the other person more than fifty percent of the time, while when they are listening, they look at the other person over seventy-five percent of the time. On the other hand, blacks tend much more to look at the person when they are talking and away from the person when they are listening. Because blacks look away more while listening, they miss some signals that require their response. The white person may think that the black isn't listening, and the black person may feel that the white person is staring at him. The result can be an uncomfortable feeling and annoyance to both black and white without either being aware of exactly why he is annoyed.

Caucasians have been found to prefer more space between speakers than blacks. When the space between speakers is increased, blacks may feel that the white person is disinterested or wishes to terminate the conversation. When the space is too close, the white person may feel that he is being intimidated or coerced by the infringement on what he feels is appropriate space for conversation.

Blacks also tend to move around more in conversation than do whites. This movement may signal to an unaware white person that the black person is restless, disinterested, or rude when such is not the case. Whites, on the other hand, tend to be less animated in conversation—to remain in a full-front position, facing the person they are talking with and only occasionally breaking eye contact. This kind of posture and contact can signal to a black that the white person is rigid, authoritarian, and intimidating and wishes to express superiority. The white, of course, is only speaking and behaving in a manner he has learned through his cultural and sociological heritage.[43]

[43]J. Fast, *The Body Language of Sex, Power and Aggression* (New York: Harcourt-Brace-Jovanovich [Jove Publications, Inc.], 1977), p. 172.

RECOGNIZING VALUES

Values are beliefs that guide and influence our actions. Because different races hold different values and because particular values affect behavior, it is essential to recognize not only the values that are peculiar to one race but also those that transcend racial and ethnic lines. Although all races in America value the basic freedoms outlined in the Constitution and Bill of Rights, our reactions to those freedoms are modified by experience as racial minorities or majorities in this country.[44] The validity of the values we hold needs to be re-examined constantly in order to make each individual flexible and receptive to understanding the values of another. This openness will diminish artificial and emotional barriers to understanding.

One must recognize the values and beliefs he holds that are blocking or promoting good interracial communication; one should avoid rejecting the value systems of another simply because of race; and one must try to discover why another's values or beliefs differ from one's own. Through a systematic examination of our own values and beliefs, we may discover that the principal barrier to interracial communication may not be different values and beliefs at all but rather the spector of emotionalism involved with race itself.

Actions and Reactions

To improve interracial communication, we must do more than simply talk about it. A positive active and reactive behavior to those of another race is absolutely essential. One must avoid attaching responsibility for racism to groups but should assign that responsibility to the individual whose behavior evinces racial prejudice. All races must set goals for overcoming differences—goals that include the avoidance of stereotyping and hasty generalization that result in polarization of the races and diminish a free exchange of information.

To reduce barriers among the races, which include "in" language and nonverbal signals that promote aggression, display a willingness to listen rather than to speak and to concede rather than to make a point. Interracial communication requires greater effort, energy, and dedication to facilitate than does communication among those of similar cultural environment. An increased awareness of the effects of our actions on the feelings of those from other racial groups is essential to promote the kind of empathetic response so necessary to modifying unsatisfactory behavior and attitudes. People of all races must become aware of the communicative factors of

[44] J. A. Blubaugh and D. L. Pennington, *op. cit.,* pp. 80–93.

physiological features, personal dress, and possessions and the use of time, space, and touch to convey nonverbal signals.

AN INDIVIDUAL PROBLEM

Interracial communication is an individual problem, born and nurtured by systematic, institutional racism. In America, we will overcome the barriers to interracial communication when we learn to trust each other, to place the sanctity and dignity of the human spirit above any ethnic loyalties or learned or felt values and beliefs, and when we are able to demonstrate by our actions that we value what an individual says, does, and is, regardless of his cultural or racial heritage.

PREPARATION = CONFIDENCE

Chapter Five

Both what one says and how he says it are of utmost importance because no matter how well one has researched and organized material, if it is not presented vividly, compellingly, and in a manner that promotes trust and confidence in the speaker, the best material will not evoke the desired reaction or productive action.[1] An oral presentation offers a speaker the opportunity to react at the time of presentation, to enhance communication by projection of attitudes, nuances of physical reaction, and tonal coloration of language through changes in force, pitch, and tempo. Oral presentation has the advantage of immediate audience feedback, and a good speaker adapts his presentation to that reaction.

Were this instant reaction not important, one could simply mimeograph the intended message, pass it out, pause for an appropriate time while people read it, and ask for reaction. One might not even convene the meeting at all but rather send the communication to individuals at their desks and then ask for written comment. Both written and oral communication are useful, but the advantage of face-to-face confrontation and the opportunity to support language physically is undeniable.

[1] See "Note on Trustworthiness" in the Appendix.

ATTITUDE

Many managers are reluctant to expend the time, effort, or energy required for preparation and presentation of a speech. Some fear adverse judgments about their own personalities and competence as managers. Public speaking is one of the best opportunities for any manager to display his competence, integrity, and his point of view; it offers an intimate insight into his personality. The speaker will project a strong and vibrant personality when he is confident that he has prepared well, that what he has to say is worthwhile, and that positive action will ensue as a result of his remarks.

Overconfidence, of course, is a sign of arrogance easily detected in a lack of preparation, a paucity of ideas, faulty organization, and failure to respond to oral or visual signaling from the audience. The overconfident speaker is concerned only with himself and what he has to say. His inept presentation will quickly earn him the dislike and disrespect of the audience and no second invitation to speak. A thoughtful, skilled communicator develops the kind of confidence, through preparation and practice, that enables him to incorporate all of his skills to support his ideas.

STAGE FRIGHT

The first step in establishing confidence as a public speaker is to overcome the fear of speaking. Personally, in twenty years of teaching and public speaking, I have never known an individual who really cared about the public-speaking situation, who did not admit to a certain amount of nervousness before speaking. This fear of speaking before others is often described with the theatrical term "stage fright."[2]

Fear of speaking is a discomfort that can be overcome and used to the speaker's advantage, for the physiological responses to fear, anxiety, and excitement are similar as the body prepares chemically to perform an anticipated action that may be unpleasant or pleasant. The public speaker must control this physiological response in order to make his presentation reflect his competence. Control of stage fright frees the speaker from depressing and distracting feelings and actions that minimize his effectiveness.

When one is preparing for a difficult task, the body metabolism causes extra adrenalin to be secreted in the bloodstream, along with thyroxin. This raises the blood pressure, which in turn increases respiration and causes the nervous response to quicken. The public speaker who notes this chemical reaction, which may cause his hands to tremble or his knees to shake, may think, "Oh, my God, am I getting nervous!"

[2]C. W. Lomas and R. Richardson, *Speech: Idea and Delivery* (Boston: Houghton Mifflin, 1956), pp. 3-5 and 40.

The very act of recognizing the nervousness causes a further chemical reaction, which makes him still more nervous. This misdirected response, if not controlled, can eventually cause a complete breakdown and can be so disconcerting and embarrassing to the speaker and to his audience that he may be discouraged from further public presentation. Recognition of what stage fright is and how to control it will, in the long run, enable the speaker to utilize this extra energy to be more effective.

Remember that most stage fright diminishes rapidly after the speaker begins to talk, and that if he didn't have some stage fright, he probably would not have cared enough about the situation to prepare. Hanawalt and Butler[3] report that an audience may stimulate the speaker's memory rather than diminish it. Therefore, when one has properly prepared and has geared his comments to an audience that he has analyzed, he will be stimulated by their reaction to extend rather than to restrict his presentation.

Anxiety or stage fright occurs when the speaker is unsure of his ability to fulfill the requirements of his assignments; he wants to do well, but he is afraid that he won't. The second step in controlling stage fright, then, is to reconcile this personal divisiveness—to unify what one is required to do, what one intends to do, and what one does.[4] This resolution of conflict enables the speaker to stop thinking of himself—how he looks, how he sounds, and what the audience will think of him—and to concentrate instead on communicating his ideas in the most purposeful and skillful way. The development of confidence in one's ability to fulfill the assignment of speaking begins when one chooses the topic and follows through with the preparation and delivery.

Adopt A Behavioral Model

More than several years ago, as an undergraduate, I discovered an invaluable technique for preparation: when I have a speech to make, I think of someone whom I admire very much and ask myself how this person would fulfill the assignment. The image of this individual's competence and his character are constantly before me as I research, synthesize, organize, and rehearse. By concentrating on how someone else might present ideas, I free myself from doubts about my own effectiveness. This use of a behavioral model allows me to stand somewhat apart from myself and to evaluate more clearly the anticipated effectiveness of the speech. I adapt my own personality to the speaking situation in an effort to gain the same kind of reaction that I have observed in my model's audience. In short, I ask

[3]N. G. Hanawalt and K. F. Butler, "The Effects of an Audience on Remembering," *Journal of Social Psychology* 29, 259–272.
[4]A. H. Maslow, *Motivation and Personality* (New York: Harper, 1954), p. 234.

myself, "Would this kind of preparation and presentation be acceptable to the person whose ethics and demeanor I have chosen to be my guide?"

Describe the Experience

It may be comforting to know that stage fright decreases with age, experience, and practice and that it is not nearly as obvious to an audience as to the speaker.[5] Much stage fright is caused by previous embarrassing situations and the desire not to "make a spectacle of myself again." To overcome this fear of repeating an error, recall the situation as vividly as possible and describe it in detail to a counselor, speech consultant, or sympathetic friend. Very likely, in this discussion, you will conclude that the incident was not very important at all, and indeed you both may get a good laugh from recalling it; you may also receive some suggestions about how to avoid such incidents in the future. The best way to counter any feeling about past failures is to experience success from a speech well prepared and well presented.

Be the Expert

A good speaker chooses a subject in which he has a vital interest. Then he researches, synthesizes, and organizes the speech until he is certain that for the few minutes that he speaks he is the foremost expert in that room—he knows more about the subject than does anyone else—and that, thanks to his preparation, the audience is going to become more informed. He rehearses the sequence of his ideas alone until it becomes almost a reflex recall. He goes over the ideas—using many different words and phrases to make them pictorially alive. He rehearses the sequence of ideas with a friend or in front of a mirror or on a tape recorder. He may go to the room where he is going to speak in order to rehearse on the podium and to test the acoustics. The good speaker leaves as little as possible to chance.

Relax

Here is a method of overcoming anxiety that I discovered years ago as an actor and college athlete: Recognize and isolate the particular anxiety; concentrate intently on its causes; then let it go. *Think of the anxiety as a physical object you can see, touch, and hold—visualize it vividly and grasp it with all your strength—then thrust it from you.* Using one's imagination to convert the anxiety into a physical metaphor (mine is a black polished ball) is the key. If you may think of anxiety as an intruding psychic fluid fill-

[5]T. Clevenger, Jr., "A Synthesis of Experimental Research in Stagefright," *Quarterly Journal of Speech,* 45, 186–197.

ing your body, you can start at the center of your head and force the fluid to drain slowly down through your body and out through the tips of your toes.

This technique takes only a minute and reduces tension faster than any other method I have found. The more one practices this procedure, the more effective it becomes.

Remember: *Recognize—visualize—concentrate—*and *eliminate!*

In the moments immediately before you speak, avoid thoughts about yourself. Concentrate on what the other speaker is saying, for you may find that you want during your own presentation to refer to something that he has said; this form of flattery compels attention. You may want to think about the reaction you desire from the audience, but the few minutes before you speak are not the time to review your organization. If you have prepared properly, when it is your time to speak, the ideas will flow as reflex actions.

WHAT TO MEMORIZE

Don't memorize a speech unless you are so skillful that you can convince an audience that you have not memorized. One of the dangers in memorizing is that force, pitch, and tempo tend to become patterned and therefore sound "sing-song." A second danger, of course, is that you may forget. A good speech, in delivery, creates what the great American actor William Gillette called "the illusion of the first time."[6] That is, the speaker should appear as an intelligent, competent, prepared individual who is uttering *these words* for *this audience* specifically.

The only parts of the speech that should be memorized are possibly the introduction, the conclusion, and any sections that must be stated in exact language to achieve full effectiveness. Undoubtedly, some parts of the speech will be memorized through practice. When the speaker finds a patterned delivery ensuing as a result of memorization, he should rephrase that section of the speech in order to maintain freshness.

---

[6]William Hooker Gillette (1853–1937) adapted the first nine Conan Doyle's *Sherlock Holmes* stories into dramatic form. He played the central character in all of these plays and received critical acclaim until his retirement in 1932. Gillette was able to compel audience attention throughout an entire production by his intense concentration and the understatement of his characterization. He was America's first truly naturalistic actor.

ORGANIZE IDEAS

Chapter Six

The value of preparation for oral communication is often overlooked because many managers feel that speaking is as natural an activity as sleeping or eating; they may be confusing quantity with quality. Careful, detailed, copious preparation saves time for everyone.

ELEMENTS OF SPEECH

Formal public speaking involves six basic factors: (1) the occasion—which makes speech desirable, (2) the speaker, (3) the oral presentation—which includes selected language, emphasis, facial expression, and gestures, (4) the audience, (5) the audience response, and finally (6) the speech text—which should be composed of significant ideas arranged in a clear and special order.[1]

SELECT THE TOPIC

The first step in preparing a speech is to select a topic. When doing this keep in mind the following:

1. Choose a topic of which you have some knowledge.
2. Choose a topic in which you have some interest and conviction.

[1]O. T. Oliver, H. P. Zelko, and P. D. Holtzman, *Communicative Speech* (New York: Holt, Rinehart and Winston, 1962), pp. 3-26 and 112-141.

3. Choose a topic that is in keeping with the interest and intellectual capacity of the audience.

4. Choose a topic that is adaptable to the time limits of the speech.

5. Choose a topic that is appropriate for the occasion.[2]

DETERMINE THE PURPOSE

After the speaker has chosen his topic, he must decide which of three general purposes or goals he wishes to accomplish: to inform, to persuade, or to entertain. This does not mean that an informative speech might not also be entertaining; and a persuasive speech is apt to be informative and might also include elements of entertainment; no speech is designed purely to persuade, entertain, or inform. Within the confines of the general purpose, the speaker can determine his specific purpose—exactly what he wishes to accomplish and what means he will use to develop the speech and support his conclusions.

To Inform

The requirements of the informative speech dictate that the speaker promote clarity, interest, and understanding. Of these three goals, clarity is the most important because if the speech is not clear, the audience will not undersand what is being discussed, and the speech will be of little interest. Clarity is vital if the speaker is giving instructions, demonstrating a process, or explaining a theory; it is especially important when the general purpose of the speech is to inform.[3]

To Persuade

Goals for the speech to persuade are to stimulate, to gain assent, and to move to action. A speaker may stimulate the thoughts and feelings of an audience by extolling those who contributed—perhaps even their lives—for the cause the speaker wishes to promote.

Speeches to persuade make direct appeals to the emotions of the audience, and this emotional appeal is used to enhance conviction and stimulate action. A salesman attempts to convince a buyer that his product is better than that of his competitor; a lawyer seeks a favorable verdict for his client; a teacher urges that his students learn significant material; and a

[2]C. G. Hurst, Jr., and L. H. Fenderson, *Effective Expression* (Columbus, Ohio: Charles E. Merrill, 1966), pp. 67–94.
[3]R. S. Ross, *Speech Communication* (Englewood Cliffs, N.J.: Prentice-Hall, 1965), pp. 119–127.

manager persuades his staff to be more efficient in fulfilling their obligations to the organization. *Action* is the goal of persuasion.[4]

The purpose of the speech to inform is to promote understanding; the purpose of the speech to persuade is to motivate the audience to believe or to do something; the purpose of the speech to entertain is to help the audience escape from reality.

To Entertain

The specific goals of the speech to entertain are interest, enjoyment, and humor.[5] The speech to entertain is the most difficult to give, because the speaker must develop an idea in a light, pleasant, friendly manner. Unfortunately some speakers think of the speech to entertain as merely involving a series of unrelated stories or jokes; however, it is vital that behind the series of stories or jokes, the speaker have a specific purpose for giving this particular speech and a body of detailed information to support that purpose.

ORGANIZATION

Once the speaker has chosen his topic and has decided on his general and specific purpose, the next step is to develop a plan or outline that details the order in which material will be presented.

The speaker can more readily hold the attention of the audience when he presents ideas organized in understandable fashion, filled with signals and signposts that demonstrate progress and constantly remind the audience of what is intended (his purpose). A well-reasoned outline divides a speech into logical parts, shows the relationship between each section and the next, and relates all parts to the conclusion.

Structuring an outline makes the speaker more assured because he is not likely to leave out an important point. Coherence will ensue because the ideas will fit together more logically. When the speech is logically organized, it is easier for the speaker to remember and for the audience to follow. When it is easy for the audience to listen, their interest and attention will be maintained, and the desired reaction is much more likely to occur. A good outline also provides a permanent record of what was covered should one have to give the same speech on another occasion.

[4]H. W. Willingsworth and T. Clevenger, Jr., *Speech and Social Action* (Englewood Cliffs, N.J.: Prentice-Hall, 1967), pp. 192–198.

[5]A. N. Monroe and D. Ehninger, *Principles and Types of Speech,* 6th ed. (Glenview, Ill.: Scott, Foresman, 1967), pp. 348–371.

A speech outline saves time by pointing up mistakes and weaknesses in both content and organization. It is much easier and less time-consuming to revise the text before the speech is in final form.

Several years ago a young lawyer wishing to go into politics asked an aging senator how best to present his material to an audience. The senator replied, "Tell them what you're gonna say, say it, tell them what you said, and sit down!" What the senator was doing was outlining the three principal structures in the development of the speech—the introduction, the body, and the conclusion.

THE INTRODUCTION

The audience gains its first *intellectual* impression of the speaker during the introduction, and this first impression can be vital to the success of the speech.[6] An accomplished speaker achieves four things in his introduction:

1. He gains attention.
2. He establishes good will.
3. He orients the audience by providing background information.
4. He clearly states his specific purpose.

Attention

There are several ways to gain attention. Humor is commonly used, but this has many pitfalls. Some people just can't tell a funny story and make it sound funny; others have a warped sense of appropriateness and good taste; and some through ineptitude, alienate the audience. A humorous story used for attention must relate to the topic, otherwise the audience may be thinking about the story when the speaker has already gone on to the next point.

Some speakers prefer to gain attention by starting with a question. This device is effective because it stimulates the audience to answer the question in their own minds. Caution: in using questions in the introduction, be prepared for unexpected responses that may require some modification of the planned presentation.

A startling fact frequently is used in the introduction to gain attention. This fact may be statistical, or it may merely be an unusual statement. The use of a startling statement to gain attention is even more effective if the element of recency is involved. Consider appropriate reference to a statement made by a previous speaker on the program.[7]

[6]C. H. Weaver, *Speaking in Public* (New York: American Book Company, 1966), pp. 228–246.
[7]*Ibid.*

Good Will

Once the speaker has gained attention, he must then establish good will. Always recognize that there are two sides to every issue, and by conceding a point to the opposition when it is obviously very hostile, the speaker may enhance his chance of a fair hearing. If the audience is strongly opposed, making people realize that they have something in common with the speaker is an affirmative step in establishing good will and common ground. Common ground may be achieved by referring to a previous experience that has been shared or by mentioning that the speaker is from the same state or county as the audience or is acquainted with someone whom the audience knows and respects. Although these techniques may not immediately promote mutual understanding, they establish a climate in which understanding is possible.

Most audiences enjoy a compliment and react favorably as long as the compliment does not become obvious flattery. Strive to mention examples of mutual achievement or areas of special interest. The good speaker establishes the impression that the audience's interests are the same as his own.

Orientation

Although it is extremely important in the introduction to gain attention and establish good will, you must also orient the audience to the subject. Give some background information on the topic; never assume that everyone is completely familiar with or knows the same amount of information. Unless the audience starts with a common understanding or background, some of the things said later will be meaningless. Definition of technical terms or special jargon used in the speech, background about events that resulted in the invitation to speak, and reference to the timeliness or urgency of the situation are good methods of orienting the audience.

Specific Purpose

The less effort an audience has to exert in listening, the more meaning the speech is going to have for them. It is much easier for an audience to listen if the purpose has been clearly stated. Statement of purpose in a speech may involve some foreshadowing in which the main points are suggested. This foreshadowing, or preview of what is to come, can make it easier for the audience to follow the sequence of development.

Because of the importance of the introduction, it is advisable to write it out completely in paragraph form so that it may be analyzed to ascertain if it meets all of the basic requirements: does it gain attention, establish good will, orient the audience, and state the purpose?

THE BODY

The function of the body of the speech is to organize logically in outline form the sequence of ideas that develop, illustrate, or illuminate the specific purpose of a speech. The material used in development may be information gained from personal knowledge and experience or from research.

The first step in preparing the body of the speech is to list all the ideas or material that you have gathered. Order or relative importance should not be considered at this time; brainstorm until everything is listed that should be included. The next task is to put these ideas into a form that is useful and meaningful to an audience, and this function is best accomplished by structuring a good outline.[8]

Frequently the speaker discovers that he has so much material or so many ideas that preparing an outline looks like a hopeless task. Should this happen to you, eliminate material in order to fit it into the time limits. Retain only those elements that appeear vital to fulfilling the purpose. Some items may be eliminated; perhaps some can also be combined. The outline will help to reduce the amount of material to a workable number of items. When the purpose of the speech has been clearly defined, the way the supporting items fit together will become more apparent. In a speech of ten to thirty minutes, probably no more than three to five main points should be considered; they must clearly support and develop the specific purpose of the speech. All subordinated material should clearly relate to and support each main idea.

Unity

The principles of good order are then: unity, coherence, and emphasis. Aristotle in his *Poetics* said that a play must be so constructed that omission of any part damages the whole and that each part of a plot must contribute to making the purpose or conclusion inevitable.[9] Each part of a speech should also contribute to the inevitability of the specific purpose or the conclusion of a speech. The material should be unified to the point that it can be summarized in a single statement of purpose. This unity is the first principle in structuring the parts of the speech. Unity assures that any material that is not part of the speaker's purpose is eliminated from the outline.

[8]Monroe and Ehninger, *op. cit.,* pp. 28–34.
[9]Aristotle, *Poetics—Ethics,* trans. S. H. Butcher and R. Williams (Chicago: Henry Regnery, 1949).

Coherence

The second principle of organization—coherence—refers to the specific sequence of the parts of the speech. Coherence—the principle of order and arrangement—shows a clear and definite relationship between each part of the speech. Do not assume that what is logical to the speaker will be logically understood by the audience. Establishing coherence between the ideas in the speech is an important step in establishing and maintaining a favorable relationship with the audience. Not only must audience members be able to recognize the logical progression of thought, but they must also distinguish the relative importance between each of the ideas. In emphasizing and developing ideas, consider carefully the use of connecting transitions or phrases. Brief phrases, such as "in the meantime," "for example," "as we have seen," "on the contrary," "to continue," and "as I have said," are useful, but also consider bridges of a more extended nature in order to avoid the trite and thereby enhance and vitalize style in presentation.

Emphasis

The next principle of organization is emphasis, which involves the arrangement of ideas in order of their importance so that each stands out clearly. Two ways of emphasizing ideas are by position and by proportion. The most emphatic positions in the speech body are at the beginning and at the end. More emphasis may also be placed on an idea by giving it more space, more verbiage. This method is called emphasis by proportion.

Order

Speeches are organized chronologically, logically, topically, spatially, in order of difficulty, and with a "need–plan" structure.[10] A chronological order involves an arrangement of ideas according to the order in which a number of events took place. The logical method of organization is closely related to the chronological; however, this method goes further in that it involves accepting cause-and-effect relationships. The cause-and-effect method is especially useful in preparing a persuasive or argumentative speech. Some material (that used for informative speeches) might be better organized by the topical method in which material is arranged according to general topics and headings. A speaker might organize spatially if he intends to discuss "Agriculture in the United States" by dividing the country into its chief agricultural areas and then describing the crops peculiar to each area.

The fifth type of general organization—by difficulty—is one in which

[10]Monroe and Ehninger, *op. cit.,* pp. 224-240 and 264-317.

problems and principles are explained, or solutions offered, in order of their complexity. The difficulty method is well-suited to an informative speech, but it is not too useful in a persuasive speech. The need–plan method in which one starts with a problem and offers solutions works very well for the persuasive speech.

OUTLINE FORM

When the method of organization has been chosen, the next step is to order the material in outline form. Two basic types of outlines are used; of these, the detailed outline is more useful to the speaker in the actual preparation of the speech while the abridged outline is more useful in the actual presentation of material.

Detailed Outline

The detailed outline, or "complete sentence outline," requires complete sentences for both main headings and subheadings. The theory, of course, is that complete sentences make for complete thoughts, and therefore require the speaker to think completely through the structure of his speech.

Abridged Outline

The abridged outline—sometimes called a "topic" or "key word outline"—does not employ complete sentences but rather uses phrases or words. With fewer details the abridged outline is easier to keep in mind and is less cumbersome to handle during the actual oral presentation of material.

In order clearly to recognize, establish, and develop main ideas with supporting detail, statistics, personal examples, and other material, outlines should be structured with a numbering and lettering system which clearly connotes subordination. Roman numerals indicate the main ideas; capital letters, the subheadings; and Arabic numbers the sub-subheadings. Consistent structure in outlining helps both the speaker and the audience.

The following speech principles are arranged in two logical outline forms using first a detailed structure (I and II) and then an abridged method (III, IV, V) to point out clearly the relationship of subordinated material to ideas used in supporting a specific purpose.

Specific Purpose: To present the basic principles of organizing material for public speaking.

I. Gather and Sort Material
   A. List everything, regardless of order or importance.
   B. Reduce the amount of material.
      1. Eliminate unnecessary items.
      2. Combine similar items.

II. Consider the principles of ordering and arranging material.
   A. Unity is the first principal of order.
      1. It defines the purpose of the speech.
      2. It makes the conclusion seem inevitable.
   B. Coherence makes for a smooth flow of ideas.
      1. It indicates relationships between parts.
      2. It is achieved by good transitions.
   C. Emphasis makes the important obvious.
      1. It is achieved by position.
      2. It is achieved by proportion.

III. Methods of organizing
   A. Chronological
   B. Logical
   C. Topical
   D. Spatial
   E. Difficulty
   F. Need–Plan

IV. Types of outlines
   A. Detailed
      1. Complete sentences
      2. Used in preparing speech
   B. Abridged
      1. Phrases or words
      2. Used in delivering speech
   C. Combination of detailed and abridged

V. Logical arrangement
   A. Main heading
      1. Three to five
      2. Indicate by Roman numerals
   B. Subheadings
      1. Principle support
      2. Indicate by capital letters
   C. Sub-subheadings
      1. Development techniques
      2. Indicate by Arabic numbers

THE CONCLUSION

For many speakers, the conclusion is the most troublesome part of a speech. Most people don't know how to stop; they don't know how to get from the main body of the speech to the conclusion. The conclusion should be a natural ending—not an abrupt halt—and this requires a good transition. The speaker tells the audience the purpose of his speech in the introduction; in the body of the speech he develops and carries out this purpose. Avoid the trite expressions "in conclusion" and "in summary" because such phrases weaken the conclusion by belaboring the obvious. The conclusion should be positive and reassuring to the audience. If the conclusion is weak, it will weaken the whole speech because this is the final impression that the audience takes with it.

The conclusion should be shorter than the introduction. Although most audiences prefer a straightforward conclusion, this does not preclude the use of appropriate quotations or mention of an incident or experience. You may ask for action or reinforce a specific point,[11] but never introduce new ideas in the conclusion! The introduction of new ideas in the conclusion offers distractions that invariably confuse.

A summary of the highlights of the speech, for purposes of re-emphasis and review, is the safest and most direct way of concluding. The speech intended to persuade may have in the conclusion a specific plea for action. If action is asked for, it should be simple and direct—something that can be quickly and easily accomplished by the audience as a first step toward achieving the overall purpose of the speech.

[11]R. R. Windes and A. Hastings, *Argumentation and Advocacy* (New York: Random House, 1965), pp. 223–238.

USE
EFFECTIVE
LANGUAGE

Chapter Seven

The chief characteristic of good communication is control. Control is the result of systematic gathering of information, precise organization of that information, attention to detail in using appropriate techniques in presentation, and selecting language that is vivid, descriptive, and adapted to the audience and to the occasion.

The speaker's style is vividly conveyed through a variety of nonverbal signals that include posture, dress, vocal inflections, and general deportment and demeanor. Style is further defined and refined by the speaker's choice of words.

Style is not simply the final polish or veneer that one presents to the public; it is rather a fusion of experience, growth, depth of thought, and sensitivity to one's culture and environment. Good style in public speaking is enhanced by well-chosen language, systematically organized and vigorously delivered for the purpose of satisfying the needs of a selected audience.

Language is the material that makes the embroidery of our minds substantial; it permits us to translate thoughts into meaning and thereby links one person to another. It is our chief intellectual tool of communication; it is used to describe experience and technique; it is used to make clear desires and wishes and to conceal feelings. Language enhances our sociability because it promotes common interests and defines purpose. Leadership emerges when one individual can clearly manipulate language to facilitate enlightenment and persuade others to action.

VOCABULARY

Knowledge is not really knowledge until it is communicated to another individual. A person who "knows what he means but can't really say it" probably doesn't know at all; he hasn't taken the time fully to formulate his idea and translate it into meaningful language. Hasty thinking generally results in hazy expression. As a first step in achieving mastery of language, a manager should work daily to increase his vocabulary. Each individual has a vocabulary that he regularly uses and one that he recognizes. More words that are recognized but not generally used should be studied, understood, and incorporated in daily communication. The more words one knows well, the better one can express his ideas.[1]

Abstract words should be defined in the context in which they are used because, as we know, individuals interpret words in the light of their own background and experience. Precise definition then is the keystone to clear understanding.

Metaphor

Metaphor may be used as an element of definition to compare the known to the unknown, but caution is advised because generalized meaning through continuous use of metaphor may result in confusing contradictions and inconsistencies. What, for example, is a "sharp comment" or a "hot time"? I once knew a minister who referred to birds as "God's feathered choir" and to a railroad as "a great boulevard of steel." Although such figurative language may invoke an intended imagery, the true meaning of the term or phrase is often lost through audience interpretation. Words should be chosen for their clarity and their ability to invoke mental pictures in the minds of the audience.

Transitions

Connective words not only furnish transitions between ideas but convey very real meanings of their own. "On," "by," "but," "or," "until," "therefore," and "however," when misused can turn a clear statement into nonsense—for example, "He was a very good athlete *but* scored many points" or "She is very responsible; *however,* she types 200 words a minute." Sensitivity to careful selection of transitions and their implications produces

[1]G. Wiseman and L. Baker, *Speech: Interpersonal Communication* (San Francisco: Chandler, 1967), pp. 93–100.

a smooth, meaningful flow of language. Misuse of transitions frequently signals a confused mind. Words that connote an association between an object or idea and its purpose and those that link causes with effects and effects with causes are concrete building blocks of attention and comprehension.[2]

Summaries

Summaries and transitions are signposts of progress; as such, they should grow naturally from the subject matter of the speech. Audiences are reassured by a feeling of progress and by being reminded of the development of the main ideas as indicated by internal summaries and the speech conclusion.

Questions

Questions within a speech text are structural devices that must also be carefully phrased. Rhetorical questions do not require a voiced reply but do evoke a predictable response from the audience if the audience is even slightly inclined toward the speaker's point of view.[3] Although the rhetorical question can be an effective device, it should be used sparingly because those who agree with you will not want constantly to reaffirm their beliefs and those who disagree with you will respond negatively. Direct questions are usually intended as opportunities for the speaker to answer himself, but one danger in using direct questions is that some members of the audience may choose to answer your question in a manner that you did not anticipate and will require you to modify your presentation on the spot. Often I have used anticipated questions as a principal structural element of a speech, thus answering the questions before they are asked.

The Best Word

One should constantly attempt to build his vocabulary by looking in the dictionary for the meanings of words he does not know, by checking a thesaurus for synonyms that may be substituted for words one uses repeatedly, by reading good literature and understanding it, and by modeling language choice after successful speakers. Some people even employ a rather mechanical device for increasing their vocabulary; they incorporate a new word in their conversation each day for a year.

[2]H. W. Ellingsworth and T. Clevenger, Jr., *Speech and Social Action* (Englewood Cliffs, N.J.: Prentice-Hall, Inc., 1967), pp. 57–80.
[3]W. P. Sanford and W. H. Yager, *Principles of Effective Speaking,* 6th ed. (New York: Ronald Press, 1963), p. 173.

STYLE

The conscientious individual asks himself if he has stated his idea as exactly, as colorfully, and with as much emotional impact and force as is appropriate. If the answer is negative, then he searches for other words and phrases to frame and structure the presentation. Carefully chosen words, while obvious symbols of erudition, must never be used as an arrogant display of accomplishment but rather for what they are—symbols for ideas and signposts for understanding.

Good language in a speech says the most in the fewest words.[4] It provides a feeling of forward movement. It has rhythm and cadence. Good oral language is both vivid and exciting; it invokes an emotional response from the audience that in turn reinforces the intellectual reaction. Good language is addressed to a specific audience, at a specific time and place, and has the quality of naturalness and appropriateness. Oral language is usually more informal than written language and makes greater use of contractions, personal pronouns, repetition, restatement, rhetorical questions, and perhaps some colloquialisms and current slang that a particular audience understands and appreciates. Oral language, appropriately chosen, has an informality and structure that promote the illusion of conversation—well-reasoned conversation, to be sure. It has directness that makes people in an audience feel that they have an opportunity and perhaps a responsibility to respond to and to participate in the communication process.

The Conversational Mode

Good conversation, of course, is free from clichés, jargon, slang, and pretentious language that is remote and impersonal. Good conversational delivery eliminates such weak expressions as "You know," "And so on," "Take and do," "kinda," and "sorta," and it banishes that dreadful example of nonfluency—the articulated pause usually expressed by "uh." The arrogance of an individual who feels that he can hold the attention of another simply by making a sound and saying nothing is incomprehensible and extremely annoying to this writer. The articulated pause results from an impression that we must continue to make sound in order to compel attention. This is not an accurate and verifiable principle of communication. The pause can be very meaningful when it has been planned for effect, and it need not be articulated by a meaningless "uh," "ya see," "eh," or "ya know." The poised speaker uses the pause in order to allow the audience to reflect, to emphasize what he will say next, or as a timing device that by breaking the rhythm and flow of his delivery maintains audience interest.

[4]D. C. Bryant and K. R. Wallace, *Oral Communication,* 4th ed. (New York: Appleton-Century-Crofts, 1969), pp. 232–249.

Moods and Emotions

Speech is pronounced and heard; therefore, the language one uses communicates moods and emotions and may modify audience attitudes.[5] Because the sounds of words so strongly affect our feelings, care in choosing words and phrases for their different tonal and rhythmic qualities is very important. Rhythm with a regular metric beat suggests solemnity; broken rhythm suggests unsureness; smooth and flowing rhythm, confidence; a gradual lengthening of phrases suggests increasing importance; and impact is intensified by presenting increasingly important concepts that lead to a climax. The variety and rhythm that word choice adds to presentation are a major contribution in the development of speaking style. One test for accurate choice of words is to check your own emotional response to the ideas that you want your words to communicate. Your response toward these images will help you select the most appropriate words for evoking response from your audience.

Loaded Words

In choosing language, avoid words and phrases that are potentially or obviously loaded in your favor—whether by the very definition or by their connotation. Avoid using leading or loaded questions, as you make your language choice relevant to the situation, the specific problem, and the individual or individuals with whom you converse. The meaning of words and phrases must be clearly understood and directed to an audience with sufficient background and experience to be able to react to the language in an intelligent manner. Language that is beyond the knowledge level of an audience embarrasses and angers listeners and may produce a reaction that is absolutely opposite of what is intended.

Writing

Bernard Shaw, the superb British playwright, once commented, "Most plays are not written, they are wrought."[6] Shaw suggested that anything creative and worthwhile required a great deal of concentration and redoing. One of the best methods of improving your use of language is to write it. You can then modify what is before you in order to pick the most exact and telling language to express your ideas. You are free to revise by striking out the dull phrase, defining fully the vague or ambiguous, and building phrases and sentences that link ideas with a continuity that leads to an appropriate climax.

[5]L. Reid, *Speaking Well* (Columbia, Mo.: Artcraft Press, 1962), pp. 178–193.

[6]R. Ohmann, *Shaw: The Style and the Man* (Middleton, Conn.: Wesleyan University Press, 1962), p. 43.

Don't be alarmed if you find yourself doing many revisions, for no one really learns without error. Error that is recognized and corrected promotes the development of a style characterized by clarity, affirmation, energy, and conviction. By writing out ideas, I am not advocating that you memorize your speech exactly, but having written out the idea completely, you will be able to recall much of the effective text when you present the speech in an "extemporaneous" manner.

The superb oral presentation is one in which the speaker has found words and phrases that gain and compel attention, promote understanding, and are acceptable and believable to the audience. These words and phrases, appropriately arranged, are then presented in a lively and vigorous manner.

DELIVERY =
COMPREHENSION

Chapter Eight

Carefully researched, synthesized, and organized material will not be well received by the audience if it is poorly delivered. Speakers who lack the interest, energy, and vitality to present their ideas vigorously will dissipate the value of good preparation because they bore the audience. When an audience must devote too much of its energy to listening to a poorly delivered speech, many people stop listening.

ENTERTAIN TO EDUCATE

Recently, two California psychologists and one from Southern Illinois University conducted an experiment in which they hired a trained actor to deliver a lecture to a group of other psychologists.[1] The lecture, which was composed of psychological and sociological jargon was absolutely meaningless in its content but was extremely well delivered. At the end of the lecture, the speaker received considerable acclaim from this group of trained psychologists, who should have been listening to what he said—which was nothing—and not how he said it, which was very skillfully.

To test further the premise that good delivery alone will compel attention, these same psychologists prepared two other lectures for this actor to

[1] A. Nietzke, "The Seductive Doctor Fox," *Human Behavior,* October 1974, 42–44.

deliver to two similar groups of freshman students. In one instance, the lecture was filled with purposeful and well-documented content. This lecture the actor presented as a bumbling, mumbling, unskillful, and altogether unattractive speaker. The second lecture had virtually no content but was delivered in a manner that suggested authority, preparation, competence, and a strong desire to communicate. The actor used good eye contact, thoughtful body control, and appropriate changes in force, pitch, and tempo; in short, it was a delivery that compelled attention throughout, and moreover, it entertained. Following the two lectures, standardized examinations were given to the two groups of students to test their new knowledge. It was discovered that the students gained more knowledge from the skillfully presented lecture, which was far weaker in content, than from the content-filled presentation that was poorly delivered.

This experiment is but one example to illustrate my premise that a speech must both educate and entertain to achieve its fullest impact and that content alone, no matter how vital to the audience, does not educate unless it entertains, commands attention, and makes meaning clear.

Know the Audience

Because audiences vary considerably in their likes and dislikes, it is difficult to define what might constitute a good delivery for a specific audience. However, a good speaker carefully analyzes his audience and adapts his style of presentation to what he assumes is their taste. The timing and content of the message, of course, affect the delivery. Here are some general good practices that can be adapted to virtually all situations.

Clarity

One of the first requirements of delivery is to make meaning clear. We have said earlier that definition is the keystone of understanding, but meaning consists of more than dictionary definitions. For example, consider the simple sentence "Voting is a public duty." By vocal stress, inflection, and other devices of emphasis, we can make that sentence mean many different things. To the question "What is a public duty?" we might answer, "*Voting* is a public duty." If someone says, "No, voting is not a public duty," we might reply, "Voting *is* a public duty." When someone asks for a single civic responsibility, we might say, "Voting is *a* public duty." When someone contends, "Voting is only for the privileged and educated few," we might say, "Voting is a *public* duty," and we might respond to the charge that voting is a privilege by emphasizing, "Voting is a public *duty.*" Vocal inflection and stress indeed modify meaning.

Rising inflections indicate questions; falling inflections indicate assertions. Subtle sound cues in our oral language convey different and sometimes unintended meaning, and that meaning is influenced by the attitudes the speaker brings to the situation and those he maintains throughout his presentation. His attitude about the material and the audience must be readily recognized, and it must be consistent if it is to convey the intended meaning.

In daily speech we incorporate many discrepancies between literal and intended meaning. We say, "How about that?" when we mean, "Isn't that astonishing?" We say, "Thanks a lot" when we mean, "You haven't helped at all" or "I don't appreciate your comment." In such cases, we use our voices to communicate something other than what the words indicate. Usually the audience understands quite readily the language of vocal inflection, and our meaning is understood. However, precision in language choice—and appropriate intonation—minimize the possibilities of misunderstanding.

Bernard Shaw once remarked, "There are fifty ways of saying yes, and five hundred of saying no, but only one way of writing them down."[2] Think how many ways one can say yes or no—influenced by anger, fear, or grief, for example, and you will quickly recognize the importance of communicating the appropriate attitude in support of your selection of language.

Emphasis and Attitude

Good delivery does not require an artificial emphasis that brings the same attitude, stress, and inflection to each word every time. What is desirable is that one be absolutely familiar with the content and meaning of the words and phrases chosen and then convey the intended meaning through his projected attitude about those words *in the context of the situation in which they are delivered.* When the speaker understands fully what he wishes to communicate, the subtle shades and nuances of mood and meaning apparent in changing vocal inflections add greatly to the vitality of the presentation. Dull, colorless expression is usually the result of dull, colorless impressions, and when expression is inaccurate and inarticulate, the audience perceives that the speaker does not understand or does not care about his material or his responsibility to the audience.

The speaker who is well prepared finds that standing before an audience is a highly stimulating experience. Not only does he have the satisfaction of knowing that he has prepared well to do something for someone else, but he has the added stimulation of the full attention of the group and the adventure and opportunity to modify and influence the thoughts and actions of that group.

[2]G. B. Shaw, *Preface to Seven Plays* (New York: Dodd, Mead, 1951), p. 24.

Conversational Quality

A good delivery has a certain spontaneous quality. It appears to be planned but not mechanical; the language is presented in a fashion that suggests that a thought process is occurring at the time of delivery. Good speech delivery is patterned after good conversation—which is filled with a variety of gestures, facial expressions, intensities, tempos, inflections, and pitch and is free of unusual or inordinate vocal or physical actions that call attention to themselves rather than support langauge.

Physical Response

Physical alertness in delivery is essential; the body should be fully prepared to respond in support of language. When the muscles are allowed to sag, poor body alignment results. The speaker who stands with one arm on a hip and elbow thrust out, stomach thrust forward, and shoulders stooped, will have great difficulty avoiding the dreary, monotonous vocal intonations consistent with such nonverbal signals.

The body should be fully ready to respond to the audience's reaction to your presentation. Stand with your weight evenly distributed on both feet and, if you like, with one foot toward the audience. This posture will help you feel and look more alert, and you will display more confidence. If there is a lectern, use it—but without depending on it for physical support. Place your hands in a comfortable position, but do not remain frozen. Move easily to and from the lectern, and remember that the very mass of the lectern adds psychological strength.

Keep your hands free for gestures to demonstrate emphasis and support ideas. Many beginning speakers ask, "What should I do with my hands?" My answer is always "Do nothing with them and you will probably do the right thing." By doing nothing, I mean that you need not consciously think about what gestures you might use; just let your gestures grow and flow naturally from what you say.

When practicing for a presentation, don't be afraid of excessive action; it is easy to modify or eliminate extraneous movement. Experience and the audience reaction will provide good keys to appropriate action. All action should appear to be a spontaneous reinforcement of your ideas at the time that they are voiced. Therefore, do not memorize a specific pattern of movement; invariably, such action makes for a stilted, mechanical presentation. Concentrate on communicating the idea in the best way possible and the gestures and movement that follow will have a naturalness and communicate an "illusion-of-the-first-time" that is compelling and highly attractive.

Eye Contact

If conversational directness is to be the goal in presentation, one must develop good eye contact with the audience. Speakers must know when the audience enjoys what is said and if it is responding as expected. Good eye contact is impaired by heavy reliance upon notes. Ideally, a speaker should be able to talk without notes when he is properly prepared; if he finds himself unable to do this, his notes should be only brief reminders of what he intends to say. If the speaker must refer to his notes, he should risk breaking audience contact to look at the notes but should not begin speaking until the idea is firmly in mind and he can again make good eye contact. Good eye contact is valuable to the speaker and to the listener because it offers direction and signifies confidence.

The listener tends to look where the speaker looks.[3] If the ceiling, floor, or lectern attracts the speaker's attention, it also attracts the audience's attention; people may sense wavering confidence and interpret his lack of good eye contact as an indication of disinterest, distrust, or inaccuracy in his statements.

To maintain good eye contact, search out individuals in the room. Make direct eye contact with them, but do not prolong the eye contact because this can embarrass some individuals and can make the neglected feel that you really don't want to look at them. The duration of eye contact must be such that one does not appear shifty-eyed or vague, as if attempting to recall the next idea. Shiftiness may communicate a desire not to make direct contact with members of the audience lest they detect a lack of sincerity; vagueness communicates a mental detachment and therefore is negative reinforcement.

Movement and Gesture

Movement upon the platform, gestures, and changes in vocal tone and inflection are all important elements in maintaining interest. Variety in visually and orally reinforcing ideas enables the audience to employ two senses instead of one as they react to the message. Lively, appropriate variety in platform behavior not only helps maintain attention; it promotes understanding.

There really are no rules to public presentation that cannot be broken when the speaker has a preconceived purpose in violating the rules and when a departure from the norm is in good taste. When an audience detects a sincere desire to communicate—signified by a well-chosen topic and a

[3] J. H. Henning, *Improving Oral Communication* (New York: McGraw-Hill, 1966), pp. 211-213.

clearly organized speech delivered with energy—it often remains unaware of a speaker's unusual physical or vocal mannerisms. Nevertheless, one should ordinarily strive to minimize or eliminate behavior patterns that draw attention to the person and away from the idea being communicated and those that communicate tension or stress in the speaker or make the audience nervous or restless.

Appropriateness is the key to platform behavior because it demonstrates a poise that reassures both the speaker and his listener. Most good speakers consider the opportunity to appear before an audience as an occasion to look their best. They fulfill audience expectations by being well-groomed. All suggestions made in the section on "The Semblance of Style" apply to any public appearance—with the key word being *appropriateness*.

Some general rules about gesture that will help you appear more at ease and more graceful on the platform are:

1. Do not make gestures with your arms and hands that cross the body.
2. When moving on the platform, lead with the foot closest to where you wish to go.
3. When you are on the platform, where you look directs the attention of the audience; don't look any place that you do not wish them to look.
4. Avoid the even-balanced palms-up gesture. Repetition of this visual signal suggests to the audience a juggler's posture and may indicate that your ideas lack firm control.
5. When pointing to an individual in the audience or to a visual aid, lead with your wrist rather than your finger. The index finger pointing at an individual can be offensive and is much less graceful than a gesture that ensues from the shoulder and terminates with a presentation of the full hand. Gestures made by the less dominant hand tend to be more delicate and therefore more revealing of inner states of mind; they, too, should be employed selectively.

An Affirmative Attitude

When called upon to speak, walk vigorously to the platform, pause, look at the audience, and wait until you have their full attention before you begin to speak. Physical tension and alertness facilitate emotional response and sympathetically modify the intricate small muscles that control the voice. The vigorous walk to the platform will promote good muscle tone and project an affirmative attitude that prepares both speaker and audience for an exciting experience. To further point up the value of positive physical behavior as reinforcement for feeling, consider the James–Lang Theory of Emotion.

Almost seventy-five years ago William James, the noted psychologist and philosopher—the father of pragmatism—suggested that feelings, instead of being the cause of bodily expression, are the result of it. He said:

> Everybody knows how panic is increased by flight and how the giving way to the symptoms of grief or anger increases the passions themselves—refuse to express the passion and it dies. Count ten before venting your anger, and its occasion seems ridiculous. Whistling to keep up the courage is no mere figure of speech. On the other hand, sit all day in a moping posture, sigh, and reply to everything with a dismal voice, and your melancholy lingers—If we wish to conquer undesirable emotional tendencies in ourselves, we must assiduously, and in the first instance cold-bloodedly, go through the awkward movements of those contrary dispositions which we prefer to cultivate. The reward for persistency will infallibly come, in the fading out of the sullenness or depression, and the advent of real cheerfulness and kindness in their stead. Smooth the brow, brighten the eye, contract the dorsal rather than the ventricle aspect of the frame, and speak in a major key, pass the genial compliment and your heart must be frigid indeed if it does not gradually thaw.[4]

Gestalt behavior theory supports James's contention that both outer and inner aspects of feeling are parts of a unified pattern and that if the pattern is begun with physical action that is desirable, the emotional feeling will be desirable as well.[5] It follows that positive physical response to language and situations promotes vitality and vividness of expression.

Occasionally, when confronting a difficult task, I have consciously forced myself to recall details, very specific ones, related not to the immediate task but to some past achievement—something I did very well that pleased others as well as myself. This pleasant, satisfying recollection motivates a positive, energizing response that I then am able to bring to bear on the task at hand.

SPEECH AND VOICE

A good speech voice may be described as one loud enough to be heard, sufficiently articulate to be understood, one firmly supported by diaphragmatic breathing, free from strain and tension, and possessing a pleasing quality that comes from well-balanced resonance. A good voice is often described as "American standard speech." Most radio and television announcers on the major networks affect speech patterns that employ a pronunciation, vocal inflection, and tonal form not identifiable with any particular region of the country. Nevertheless, when one is not a native of the same area as one's audience, one should not be overly concerned with

[4]W. James, *Psychology: Briefer Course* (New York: Henry Holt, 1907), p. 382.
[5]W. M. Parish, "Implications of Gestalt Psychology," *Quarterly Journal of Speech,.* 14 (1928): 8–30.

regionalisms so long as they do not interfere with communication. Vibrance is far more important than dialect.

Monotony

One of the great enemies of attention is monotony. There are many ways to be dull, but one of the most effective is to speak without changing pitch and with a constant level of intensity and timing; these create a rhythmic pattern that tends to lull. A principal method of gaining and maintaining attention, *variety* is important in what we see and in what we hear.

Breath Control

The first step in developing a good voice is to establish good habits of breath control.[6] Good breath control ensues when the diaphragmatic and abdominal muscles—rather than the muscles of the ribs and shoulders—control breathing. The diaphragmatic muscle, shaped like an inverted bowl, separates the chest from the abdomen. When the diaphragm contracts, it reduces its arch to virtually a flat plane. This allows additional air to rush into the space provided at the bottom of the lungs—which rest on the diaphragm. When the diaphragm expands, forced to do so by abdominal muscle contractions, it forces air out of the lungs and up over the vocal folds; these vibrate, creating sounds that human beings translate, through artificial manipulation called articulation, into recognizable signals called speech.

In good diaphragmatic breathing, expansion of the abdomen takes place during inhalation not exhalation. Diaphragmatic breathing will increase lung capacity and enable the speaker to carry through in one breath group, long phrases that may be necessary for the full expression of an idea; it eliminates breath-caused pauses that occasionally obscure meaning and cloud emphasis. If each day a speaker devotes a few conscious moments to the practice of good diaphragmatic breathing, this will be invaluable in gaining good breath control, which is the foundation of all vocal development and which helps project the firmness and steadiness characteristic of a self-assured and affirmative speech pattern.

Vocal Relaxation

In order to avoid a tight, pinched, hoarse, raspy, or throaty quality that connotes strain and tension, the speaker must learn vocal relaxation. Relaxation occurs when only those muscles necessary to voice production are employed. Vocal tone is produced in the larynx, which rests at the top of

[6]J. Eisenson, *Basic Speech* (New York: Macmillan, 1950), pp. 14–40.

the windpipe.[7] Changes in pitch are almost entirely due to changes in tension in the vocal folds; the thicker the vocal folds, the lower the pitch; thickness comes through relaxation.

Although it is difficult to modify one's normal pitch from soprano to bass, one can control variety in pitch by consciously contracting and relaxing the muscles that influence the production of sound. When individuals are required to speak loudly or when they are under emotional stress, they tend to tighten the muscles of the throat. What they should do is to relax them; otherwise, the tense sympathetic muscles surrounding the larynx are sure to adversely affect the quality of sound produced.

A method of relaxing vocal cords that I have found very valuable is to practice yawning. I do this for one minute in the morning before I brush my teeth and for one minute in the evening before retiring. Try this exercise and note the relaxation that follows.

Resonance

Good voice should have the characteristics of ease and relaxation but also firm support and a pleasing resonance. Proper resonance is gained when the speaker consciously manipulates the relative size and shape of the resonating cavities that influence sound. These are the mouth, the pharynx (the region just above the larynx and behind the tongue), the nasal cavity, and, to some extent, the chest. Although the ability to regulate resonators is influenced by genetic factors such as the softness of the gums, shape of the mouth, and thickness of the cheeks, voice quality can be materially improved through proper practice. Unless the speaker is tone-deaf, he will be able to eliminate harshness and a nasal twang after listening to a tape recording of his voice.

Tone

To recognize good tonality, hum the letter "m." Notice how the resonators come into play as this letter is pronounced. Copy this tonal form in pronouncing vowels. Next, pronounce "ahh" and try to feel the same resonation that you felt when you hummed "m." Try to feel the vibrations through all the resonance cavities. With a deep breath, alternate the "m" and "ahh" sound for ten seconds; increase and decrease volume without modifying resonance.[8]

It is true that for the expression of logical content, a melodious voice

[7] *Ibid.*

[8] J. Akin, *And So We Speak: Voice and Articulation* (Englewood Cliffs, N.J.: Prentice-Hall, 1958), pp. 189–199 and 205–211.

and American standard speech patterns and pronunciation are not absolutely necessary; however, vocal signals, which suggest a lack of assurance, characterized by tension and distracting misarticulation, will prove irritating to an audience and will therefore diminish the effectiveness of the speaker's presentation. A well-controlled and modulated voice will measurably assist the speaker in freeing his ideas from the bonds of monotony by enabling him vocally to reinforce and emphasize the ideas that he feels are most important.

Timing

Vocal flexibility is valuable in conveying meaning, but it is no more valuable than the element of timing. Timing consists of variations in duration and basic rate as well as the purposeful use of the pause. It matters little whether the overall rate of delivery is fast or slow; some words or phrases need to be emphasized in the general context of the speech text by modifying their time values. These variations usually are effected by lengthening a syllable or word to give the audience time fully to assimilate and to comprehend its mood and meaning. Emphasis through duration is usually combined with changes in pitch and intensity and perhaps purposeful pauses to accentuate and reinforce the full importance that the speaker accords the word or phrase.

Generally, the most effective method of indicating changes in mood or direction is by effecting a change in the rate of delivery. The average person in normal conversation speaks approximately 130 words a minute.[9] The rate, of course, may vary from 80 to 180, depending upon the situation, the other person, the subject matter being discussed, and the mood that the speaker wishes to establish.

Rate alone sometimes conveys as much meaning as language because the nonverbal signals communicated by speed, or a lack of it, are extremely strong indicators of mood, intensity, and attitude. When a speaker hurries through an idea, he may convey to the audience that this idea is not very important. On the other hand, if he lingers too long on an idea, he may give the impression that he has not fully thought it through. Rate should fit the mood, the idea, and the language chosen.

Pauses, unlike written punctuation, are inserted in a conversation as methods of suggesting mood, as a means of emphasizing words and phrases, and as transitions from one idea to another. Purposeful pauses in the middle of a speech, if the audience knows that they are planned and not the result of the speaker having forgotten what he wants to say, can be valuable and telling devices. Well-planned pauses give the audience an opportunity to reflect on the idea just presented and to gather their thoughts

[9]W. Abbot, *Handbook of Broadcasting* (New York: McGraw-Hill, 1937), p. 52.

for reception of the next idea. Selective pauses also indicate a thoughtful, assured delivery style.

Well-placed pauses help the speaker breathe properly and avoid gasping for air, which characterizes the speaker who lacks good breath control. By permitting the speaker to gather his thoughts before presenting the next idea, pauses help him avoid choppiness and the "articulated pause" mentioned earlier. Pauses should be carefully planned to reinforce and emphasize language, to enhance the speaker's poise and self-confidence, and therefore to convey meaning beyond the simple definition and explanation provided by language alone.

Intensity

The final element of voice that should be considered in delivery is intensity. Intensity involves loudness, emphasis on consonant sounds that promote clear articulation, and a recognizable change in energy during delivery. Intensity in voice gives the impression that each muscle in the speaker's body is alert and controlled and thus unified and pointed toward the expression of a particular attitude or point of view. When the elements of tempo, pitch, force, and volume are skillfully manipulated to reinforce ideas, the speaker truly is the possessor of a good voice.

PRACTICE DELIVERY

This book has previously stressed the importance of developing good speech habits and has suggested some methods of practice in preparation for delivery. Here are some other ways to enhance delivery.

In addition to becoming accustomed to the topography of the room in which one will speak, it is also an excellent idea to rehearse the speech there—moving about on the platform as one would hope to move during the actual delivery. Visualize the audience; anticipate questions and interruptions, perhaps even distractions; and practice how to accommodate and, if necessary, compensate for those interruptions. If possible, have someone—preferably a consultant—review the oral presentation in which actual presentation conditions are simulated. A trained consultant is the person who can best point out distracting mannerisms and organization that leaves meaning obscure. The consultant has the advantage of being a disinterested professional whose status is not affected in any way by your message. His sole function is to help eliminate problems that may interfere with your presenting your ideas in the clearest, most logical, most comprehensible manner.

Available Ears

Often in practicing a speech, at the dinner table I present ideas to my wife or children just to see if I am clear and logical. Although none of the members of my family are especially interested in the work I do, nor are they skilled in communication techniques, they are able to indicate, by verbal and nonverbal signals, when my meaning is clear. When it is not, I choose different words and phrases—if need be, many times, until I am certain that I have made my ideas understood.

Recording and Revision

Practice with a videotape recorder is extremely valuable. If you are sufficiently detached from your own ego to evaluate the videotape, you will find it of great assistance in correcting errors. One of the problems of attempting to evaluate a recorded presentation of one's own speech, incidentally, is that we tend to become so interested in ourselves—how we look and how we sound—that occasionally we do not listen for a clear delineation of ideas. Once more, I would suggest having the recorded speech criticized by an impartial professional.

Rehearse

Only through rehearsal can the speaker become familiar with his ideas and his material. Only through mastery of material will the speaker be able to give a clear, interesting, and compelling presentation. Take advantage of the many opportunities during the day to rehearse the sequence of ideas. You can rehearse while driving to work, while having a cup of coffee during a break, or while waiting for the next appointment. Review the sequence of ideas silently, stating them in as many different words and phrases as possible so that the sequence is firmly fixed in mind. Such a silent rehearsal is not the time to revise the order of the speech but to perfect the development of specific ideas that lead to the conclusion.

However important silent rehearsal may be, it is not as important as oral rehearsal. Too often the busy executive gets a sequence of ideas in mind, composed by himself or someone else, takes the manuscript to a meeting, and presents it for the first time before an audience. Such delivery readily reveals a lack of preparation and sometimes an arrogance and pomposity that are not reassuring to the listener.

Most people feel silly practicing an oral presentation in an empty room. However, even if a willing listener is not available, such practice can be helpful—especially if the presentation is recorded for review. For oral practice, I suggest that the speech be presented from beginning to end, rather than by repeating specific sections. Occasionally the speaker becomes so enamored of one section of his speech that he perfects that section and neglects the rest; as a consequence, he does not have a meaningful whole.

When practicing a speech, the speaker should outline the sequence of ideas in the briefest form possible; the outline should be used only to remind the speaker of what comes next. Too many details in the outline will prove distracting and cumbersome, and will cause modifications in the tempo that may carry over into the actual presentation before an audience.

STYLE

If you plan to read your speech from a manuscript, the principal difficulties in delivery are concentrating on the idea and making direct contact with the audience while still reading words from a script. In order to fix the sequence of ideas in mind in the manuscript speech, it is a good idea to write a precis that condenses the content to about one-third its actual size, memorize that content—or at least commit it somewhat to mind—and then rehearse. When one knows the organization, when one can anticipate the developmental order of support, then reading does become more direct and more spontaneous. Repeated practice in reading the manuscript will enable the speaker to look up more frequently from the text, to make better contact with the audience, and to gesture and move when it is appropriate to do so without searching for the next word on the page.

Delivery that discourages attention rather than compels it will also disguise or perhaps even conceal the value of what the speaker says. Yes, both what you say and how you say it are important, for if what you say is not said in a clear, direct, lively, and emphatic manner, your audience may not even hear, and certainly will not listen with enthusiasm and anticipation.

GROUP LEADERSHIP
AND
DISCUSSION METHODS

Chapter Nine

◄ A successful leader is a person who has mastered the art and the craft of motivating people to do what they may not want to do in such a way that they enjoy doing it. "One who can successfully redirect the self-interest of those whom he supervises" is another way of describing a leader. Character traits and patterns of behavior that clearly delineate leadership qualities are readily revealed in the dynamics of group discussion, and leadership will be conferred by the group when members recognize or gain the illusion that one of them has the power to significantly affect the well-being and actions of others. For leadership to be vested in the best qualified individual, patterns of behavior and techniques of manipulation must be understood and practiced.

TENETS OF LEADERSHIP

The leader is not necessarily the wisest, most experienced, most attractive, or most capable member of the group; he is, however, the one who can present the impression of having something unique to offer.[1] This uniqueness gives him the power to lead. The *impression* of competence and not the competence itself seems paramount in motivating the conferral of leadership. Someone may gain

---

[1]D. W. Johnson, "Communication and the Inducement of Cooperative Behavior in Conflict: A Critical Review," *Speech Monographs* 41 (1974): 64–78.

power simply when members of the group recognize his legitimate authority—either because of his title or his position in the organization or because of his designation or election as leader of the group.[2]

Leadership also emerges when members of the group express a desire to identify with a specific member.[3] Such leadership is not interpreted by the group as manipulative; it is charismatic and results occasionally from demagoguery. The collective thought of a group led by a charismatic person will be no better and perhaps no worse than that of the leader.

Leadership may assert itself when a threat or power to effect punishment is perceived by members of a group.[4] This kind of coercive leadership is effective for short-range goals and decisions but is not desirable as a managerial style that promotes the creative thought and risk-taking necessary for genuine productivity.

The desire for reward when one agrees or conforms to the leader's wishes is another strong incentive for members of the group to confer power.[5] This tentative leadership is effective only to the extent that the reward is perceived as greater than the unpleasantness caused by the assigned task. Under a system of "reward for task accomplished," the group feels controlled, perhaps even resentful, because it recognizes its own materialistic behavior, and most people like to believe that they are motivated by unselfish principles. When personal gain is the sole compensation for achievement, people feel emotionally divided between the ideal and the real.

Although reward power may elicit more positive results than coercive power because the consequences are more pleasurable, the attitude toward leadership derived principally from the tenets of power and reward are not nearly as productive as those that grow from a recognition of leadership based on expertise and credibility.[6]

Competence, trustworthiness, firmness, consistency, and a social concern seem to be the qualities that most groups desire in a leader. Through his previous actions, attitudes, and style, the expert leader has established an aura or quality of good will that encourages participation.

All methods of effecting leadership can and should be used for solving a given problem, but the leader who is recognized as an expert has a more lasting influence. Leadership exists only when it is perceived by those to be

[2]J. French and B. Raven, "The Bases of Social Power," in *Studies in Social Power,* ed. D. Cartwright (Ann Arbor, Mich.: University of Michigan Press, 1969), pp. 118–144.

[3]J. Fendrich, "Perceived Reference Groups Support: Racial Attitudes and Overt Behavior," *American Sociological Review* 32 (1957): 960–968.

[4]M. Miller, D. Butler, and J. McMartin, "The Ineffectiveness of Punishment Power in Group Interaction," *Sociometry* 32 (1969): 24–42.

[5]B. Schlenker and J. Tedeschi, "Interpersonal Attraction and the Exercise of Coercive and Reward Power," *Human Relations* 25 (1972); 427–439.

[6]M. Guldman and L. A. Frass, "The Effects of Leader Selection on Group Performance," *Sociometry* 28 (1965): 82–88.

influenced, and it is sustained only when the expert, legitimate leader has the courage and will to monitor and evaluate the contributions of the group and to reward and punish.

Evaluations of contributions by individual members, far from being demoralizing or discouraging creativity, promote teamwork and unity of purpose. Failure to evaluate results in diminished influence and a subsequent loss of leadership.

Character Traits

Social and psychological studies have helped draw a profile of the character traits generally attributed to leaders.[7] Leaders are perceived to be self-assured and confident, to have little nervous tension and greater emotional maturity, to be aggressive but sensitive to the needs of others, and to have an intelligence quotient that is above average. Leaders are adjudged willing to take responsibility, diplomatic, and persuasive in their dealings with others.

Might not leadership emerge when an average individual behaves in such a way as to suggest the qualities described above? The answer is definitely yes! One can incorporate a style in bearing and interpersonal relations that communicates all positive traits hoped for in the ideal leader. It is reasonable to assume that behavior that suggests competence, self-confidence, and a variety of other personality traits associated with leadership can be learned and projected to establish an attractive managerial style that is conducive to productivity.

Leadership Style

Managerial style ranges between that of the extreme autocrat, who makes decisions and informs the group, and that of the *laissez faire* leader, who establishes no boundaries for discussion and no goals and assumes little or no responsibility for the conclusions of the group, other than to transmit them to "higher authority."

The effective discussion leader approaches the problem of achieving consensus in one of three different ways.[8] First, he may present his conclusions to the group and tell people that they may influence him to change and

[7]M. Beer, R. Buckout, M. W. Horowitz, and S. Levy, "Some Perceived Properties of the Difference Between Leaders and Non-Leaders," *Journal of Psychology* 47 (1959): 49–56; R. Kiessling and R. Kelish, "Correlates of Success and Leaderless Group Discussion," *Journal of Social Psychology* 54 (1961): 359–363; and G. B. Bell and H. E. Hall, "The Relationship Between Leadership and Empathy," *Journal of Abnormal and Social Psychology* 49 (1954): 156.

[8]L. B. Rosenfeld, *Human Interaction in the Small Group Setting* (Columbus, Ohio: Charles E. Merrill, 1973), pp. 130–132, and R. B. Cattel and L. G. Stice, "For Formula on Selecting Leaders on the Basis of Personality," *Human Relations* 7 (1954): 195–503.

that certainly his thinking and final decision will be affected by their discussion. Or the leader may present several alternatives and ask for discussion to help formulate the best decision or course of action.

A third and perhaps the most appealing style of group leadership is for the leader simply to define the task and the ground rules for the ensuing discussion. For example, a leader may announce that production has steadily fallen off during the last six months. Obviously this cannot continue, and therefore a group discussion is necessary in order to find a solution to correct this. The group is then able (1) to recognize the problem so that it may devote its full energies to discussing possible solutions, (2) utilize its group expertise in selecting the most logical solution, and (3) decide how best to implement that solution.

In each of these discussion styles, the leader has the opportunity to get meaningful input from the group and to promote the attitude that the final decision is group-oriented.[9] This impression of group participation in the final decision increases professional pride because each member feels that he is helping "run the business"—that he does indeed influence management decisions.

A good discussion leader reflects and gives credit for all of the contributions made by the group when he makes his decisions and final report and when he takes action.

The first and second leadership styles encourage questioning and presentation of alternatives but leave the final decision to the leader. The third is obviously more democratic and likely to result in more creative and perhaps more productive action. A discussion leader who does not exercise some kind of control, either by presenting decisions and alternatives or by setting boundaries for discussion, is abdicating his responsibility for leadership and probably decreases his potential for influence within the group.

The Sargent-Miller leadership test concludes that autocratic leadership tends to promote tension and antagonism and lessens the feeling of professional worth in the members of the group.[10] Conversely, a more democratic style tends to dissipate tension and competition and therefore encourages a feeling of solidarity and professional pride in individual contributions.

Leadership requires the ability to manipulate discussion in order to arrive at a desired goal. The degree to which this manipulation is obvious is a strong determinant in recognizing positive and negative leadership qualities. The more democratic leader gives the impression that he is "people oriented" while the more autocratic leader indicates that he is more "task oriented."[11]

[9]W. Schultz, *Here Comes Everybody* (New York: Harper and Row, 1971), pp. 225–228.
[10]F. Sargent and G. Miller, "Some Differences in Certain Communication Behaviors of Autocratic and Democratic Group Leaders," *Journal of Communication* 21 (1971): 223–250.
[11]L. Rosenfeld and T. Plax, "Personality Determinance of Autocratic and Democratic Leadership," *Speech Monographs* 41 (1975): 204–206.

The task-oriented leader's influence grows largely out of his ability to effect reward and punishment, and consequently he is more likely to be a target for hostility. The people-oriented leader derives his influence from the group's desire to identify with the symbol of competent, thoughtful, courageous leadership. He receives small gifts, large responsibility, and some praise from the group. They like him because he is perceived as "one of us," but occasionally they expect him to do their "homework"—perhaps to present solutions that they feel free to accept or reject. This leader may find himself working for his constituents.

Define Goals for Constituents

In order to be a good group leader, whether task-oriented or people-oriented, the potential leader must recognize and state clearly what needs to be accomplished. He must then adapt his techniques in order to fit the personalities of the group so that he may make the most of the various talents available. A good leader knows when to encourage, when to prod, when to provide information, and when to withhold it, in short, he knows the people with whom he works. The successful group leader must firmly believe that he has the qualifications and the skill to guide and lead his group to the most logical and meaningful conclusions. He must also have the courage fully to support group recommendations and to execute the appropriate action suggested by these conclusions.

A completely autocratic and arbitrary style of leadership may be perceived by the group as effective and desirable either when a specific emergency task must be accomplished quickly or when people trust the leader. Trust is achieved when the leader has demonstrated the ability to achieve goals and still maintain, perhaps even enhance, the welfare of the individual members of the group.[12]

A competent leader is perceived by the group as predictable, courageous, flexible, and emphatic; he has zeal and sufficient communication skills to lead the group to the most logical and most advantageous conclusions and to effectively convey the wishes of the group to others. Behavior that suggests this vibrant, affirmative personality establishes a leadership style that promotes trust and confidence—the final determinants of one's ability to lead.

FACTORS OF INFLUENCE

In group discussion the good leader is aware of a variety of factors that promote or diminish communication and he utilizes them to influence the discussion.

[12]D. Cartwright and Z. Zander, ed., *Group Dynamics: Research and Theory,* 3rd ed. (New York: Harper and Row, 1968), pp. 301–317.

The Physical Environment

He knows about the nonverbal communicative significance of the room in which the group meets. He recognizes that a small, intimate room promotes interaction; that where he seats people can promote or diminish conflict; that the aesthetic qualities of the room may significantly modify the nature of discussion. For example, N. Mintz discovered that when people perceived a room in which they regularly met to be unattractive, they became bored, fatigued, irritable, and hostile and sometimes developed headaches and other psychosomatic illnesses.[13] Conversely, when group members consider the room attractive, they manifest feelings of comfort and enjoyment and exercise greater energy in their discussion.

In addition to taking into account the topography of the room, the manager considers the color of walls and the accompanying decoration—including tastefully chosen pictures or paintings. Max Luscher clearly demonstrated in 1969 that the colors people choose and reject reveal much about their personalities and that individuals tend to behave differently when confronted with different colors.[14] Blues and grays are perceived as dull and drab; these colors on walls tend to dampen conversation. Green is restful but fresh; one might reasonably conclude that discussion conducted in a room with green walls would tend toward tranquility. White is perceived as clean and efficient—pure and free from contamination; this lack of color may support a sterile or unimaginative discussion. Hues of red and orange are alive and bright, and very likely to promote vigorous interaction among the group members.

When we accept the premise that the wall colors in a room affect the feelings and moods of the individuals there, we must also conclude that the intensity of light and the color of light will have a similar effect. The cold blue of a fluorescent light tends to create a detached attitude and may even produce drowsiness. Ideal lighting for a meeting room has a tint of gold or pink and is strong enough so that participants do not have to expend extra energy in simply seeing each other. At the risk of seeming theatrical, a meeting room might have surfaces lit by somewhat different hues and intensities in order to avoid the boredom that an evenly lighted room can produce. When the eye has to adapt to different intensities and hues, this becomes a stimulating activity that promotes alertness.[15]

[13]N. Mintz, "Affects of Aesthetics Surrounding: Roman II. Prolonged and Repeated Experience in a Beautiful and an Ugly Room," *Journal of Psychology* 41 (1956): 459–466.

[14]M. Luscher, *The Luscher Color Test,* trans. I. Scott (New York: Random House, 1969).

[15]R. G. Williams, *Lighting for Color and Form* (New York: Pittman, 1954), pp. 24–38.

Members of the Group

The good manager also recognizes the innate rhythms within his group. He is aware of how people synchronize with one another. He is conscious of the best days on which to meet and the best time to meet on those specific days. Perhaps he has even drawn a profile of when people hear best, see best, and feel best—when they do their best work. Some people function best early in the morning; some, immediately before or after a meal; and some, in the evening.

When to Meet

The manager also realizes that meetings are expensive forms of communication. They require bringing together a variety of experts who might profitably be doing something else. Before any meeting is called, the manager should consider whether the meeting is really necessary—whether he could get the information by conference call, telephoning individuals, or simply walking across the hall to talk to one or two people. He should also decide if his presence is important at the meeting. If it is not, he should send a subordinate; this will save his time and give the subordinate experience. Only those people immediately concerned with the question should attend the meeting. When their presence is required for just a portion of the session, they should be so scheduled and informed to arrive and leave as needed.

How much a meeting costs can be quickly and roughly ascertained when one computes the cost of each session in terms of the salaries of those who attend. A more complete computation of cost considers the time wasted by starting a meeting late or extending it overtime and by digressions due to failure to follow a prearranged agenda. When meetings are discovered to be inordinately expensive, another form of communication, or tighter control, is in order.

The Format for Discussion

Group discussion may take several forms. The meeting can be organized as a panel, a roundtable, a conference, a symposium, or a colloquium. It can have as its purpose problem solving or the improvement of interpersonal relationships among the members. It may employ role playing, dialogue, or brainstorming techniques for promoting discussion and understanding. No matter what form a discussion group takes, what purpose for its being convened, and which techniques are used to formulate opinion, the discussion group remains the single most effective opportunity for people to share responsibilities, knowledge, skills, and attitudes and to communicate them purposefully to others.

Specific Purpose Defined

Meaningful group discussion has a specific and defined purpose and a certain procedure to guide the discussion. The delineation of both purpose and procedure is the responsibility of the group leader. He must maintain unity of purpose, avoid distracting digressions, and maintain an order and format that insure that all issues are appropriately dealt with, that all individuals are heard, that the meeting is started and concluded in the allotted time, and that final conclusions are recorded and reported to appropriate individuals within and without the group.

Although the goal of group discussion is to arrive at agreement, disagreement must not be discouraged; as a matter of fact, the group could agree to disagree completely—which may result in compromise that satisfies everyone. The group should clearly understand and agree that decisions and recommendations reported from the group bear the endorsement of all members of the group. Once a decision has been agreed upon, members should no longer feel free to demur privately or publicly. That is why disagreement within the group should not be considered undesirable but rather as a condition for promoting further discussion and enlightenment.

Cooperation

One of the favorite phrases of Lyndon Baines Johnson was "Let us reason together." Reasoning together is what discussion is all about; in order to reason together, people must adopt an attitude of friendly cooperation. It is absolutely proper for individuals to support and to defend a particular point of view in an effort to convince others to behave in the way they consider most desirable or to think the way they think; however, unsuccessful advocates of points of view or action must bend to the wishes of the group. Making inaccurate, vague, and ambiguous statements, allowing emotion to interfere with reason, and arguing against the man rather than the idea should be recognized as detrimental to consensus and be eliminated.

Deliberation

Group deliberation is simplified when the leader defines clearly the nature of the problem; the group is then free to discover, through all its resources, the best possible solution or solutions. In the course of the discussion, the group may accept or reject any number of solutions before it finally resolves the problem.

A deliberative problem has two characteristics: it is current and it is soluble. A current problem is one in which the organization is immediately and specifically concerned; a soluble problem is obviously one in which the designated group and the organization have power to act. If the problem is not current, people are not going to be interested in discussing it; if it is not soluble, there is nothing they can do about it. Once a problem is judged current and soluble, the next step is to present a variety of possible solutions. The group, through deliberation, decides which one it will adopt.

Deliberation, then, involves not only exposition—the presentation of solutions—but also the support of those solutions by research, reasoning, and documentation, which clearly point out to the group the superiority of one solution over another. It is conceivable that in arguing against the acceptance of a solution some may contend that new evils, more odious than the present problem, may ensue—for example, higher costs, less efficient operation, restriction of individual freedom, or more bureaucratic control. It is then the obligation of proponents for a given solution to argue that new evils will not arise if their proposal is adopted. Fruitful discussion will ensue when the leader has informed all discussion members of the subject, provided them with suggested reading assignments prior to the meeting (perhaps assigning individuals specific responsibilities for reporting on various issues relevant to the subject), and feels confident that the most informed experts on that particular subject are at the meeting.

Problem Solving

Most discussion groups come together for the purpose of solving problems, and the foundation of problem solving lies in preparation and analysis. John Dewey's concept of "reflective thought," which he introduced in 1933, seems to be the cornerstone on which most modern guides for group discussion depend.[16] Alan Monroe's "motivated sequence"—a system of organization that I have long employed—follows very closely the Dewey system.[17] Monroe's "motivated sequence" involves gaining attention, establishing need, satisfying that need, visualizing the consequence of acceptance or rejection of solutions presented in the satisfaction step, and then seeking action as a result of the visualization.

Regardless of the labels we place upon the thought process in group discussion, the first step is to make the group aware of the problem and the necessity of immediately dealing with it. A good group leader captures the imagination and interest of the group in order to motivate them to continue their discussion in the second stage—in which the problem is clearly defined. Definition of terms, clarity of impressions about what may have caused the

---

[16]J. Dewey, *How We Think* (Boston, Mass.: D. C. Heath, 1910), pp. 107–115. Dewey's "Model for Reflective Thinking" requires the problem to be recognized, defined, solutions suggested, solutions examined and compared, and finally a selection of the best solution—followed by testing and verification of the solution's validity.

[17]A. H. Monroe, *Principles and Types of Speech,* 3rd ed. (New York: Scott, Foresman, 1949), pp. 307–357.

problem, what forces might be resisting solutions, what resources might be called upon to assist in solving the problem, cost factors, time factors, and the criteria used to evaluate any solution are clearly important elements in defining and focusing upon the specific problem. Only when the specific problem is firmly implanted in the minds of the group is it possible to generate solutions.

When a variety of solutions have been presented, the group sets about, through analysis, to eliminate those solutions that seem less related to the defined problem. The next solutions eliminated are those that are impractical or beyond the ability of the group to handle. The remaining solutions are then carefully analyzed and evaluated to ascertain if they take advantage of the available resources, if they will encounter opposing forces, and if they are feasible in terms of cost, time, and personnel. Finally, the group considers which solutions are likely to be most acceptable to others outside the group—people who have not had the full advantage of the group's discussion. Through comparison and contrast of the positive and negative values of the remaining solutions, the best is selected.

The best solution may be chosen by consensus, by majority vote, or by a subcommittee appointed to decide the best solution based upon the discussion of the "committee of the whole." Should no single solution be supported by a majority, the leader may pick what he considers the best solution—which might be a compromise that includes many of the best features of those solutions remaining. The dynamics of the group will dictate the methods of arriving at the final decision, and any of these methods may be employed for any given problem when the leader has the trust and confidence of his group.

Once the final solution has been chosen, it is the responsibility of the group to suggest how the solution will be implemented and how it will be evaluated. Both successful implementation and thorough evaluation are necessary in order to test the validity of any course of action.

The Discussion Topic

The discussion format may be rigid or flexible, but a good manager and discussion leader must carefully choose a topic which is well-suited to the group. A topic clearly defined and analyzed motivates support for various contentions and limits divergent attitudes that may result in hostility and conflict. When the topic is clearly understood and each person has had his say, the group is more willing to implement and evaluate the chosen solution and to share the leader's responsibility and accountability for success or failure.

HANDLING CONFLICT

The principal method of avoiding conflict is to keep the group goal-oriented—constantly to keep before them the general and specific purpose for meeting. What happens when alternative solutions of equal worth and attractiveness are presented? What happens when only distasteful—but necessary—solutions emerge? What happens when alternative solutions emerge that combine the pleasant and the unpleasant?

Conflict is a completely natural activity. It is a healthy activity that promotes creativity and forces people to defend their positions and to strive for what will most benefit them and perhaps, in the long run, the organization. Conflict should be avoided only when it is nonproductive—when it causes such a rent in the group and divergence in the discussion that the goal is obscured. Conflict that includes personal attacks on various members of the group destroys group cohesiveness and may instill in group members such hostility and aggression that progress toward compromise is impossible.

Conflict is to be encouraged when it is properly managed—for conflict promotes involvement and commitment.[18] Conflict, skillfully managed, develops methods for coping with different opinions and personalities and may thus furnish the firm foundation for an understanding—an *esprit de corps* so necessary for organizational teamwork. Resolved internal conflict clears the air of "hidden agendas," destructive *non sequiturs* that destroy meaningful discourse, and allows the group to focus upon the most logical, feasible, and productive solutions to problems.

When conflict is unresolved or suppressed by the leader, it is likely to result in hidden and smoldering resentment of a decision that some members feel was forced upon them—one that they agreed to because they feared the censure of the leader or the displeasure of the majority or because they thought that others had concluded that their contributions were not worthwhile.

Conflict produced by forces outside the group is extremely useful because it allows the leader to focus on an enemy from without and to muster the entire resources of the group to solve a given assigned problem. Such conflict may, however, be counterproductive if the group cannot solve the problem.

Bach and Wyden, in their book *The Intimate Enemy,* point out that many members of a group avoid productive conflict by refusing to deal directly with the problem lest they risk self-exposure.[19] Such people may

[18]R. L. Johannesen, *Ethics and Persuasion* (New York: Random House, 1967), p. 102.
[19]G. R. Bach and P. Wyden, *The Intimate Enemy* (New York: Avon, 1968), pp. 97–114.

leave the room when conflicting viewpoints are presented, remain in stony silence, or decline to support either of two points by saying that both are good. They may also change the topic to a more neutral one, thus avoiding any contention, or they may make a joke of the total discussion, saying, "Let's keep everybody happy."

Other methods of resisting the demanding requirements of group discussion are included in what Paul Thorensen calls "fight defenses and flight defenses." Fight defenses operate on the premise that "the best defense is a good offense." This behavior is engaged in by individuals who spend their energies and a great part of a meeting using parliamentary gymnastics in attempts to outshine the leader.

These same people express cynicism about the ability of the group to deal with the problem and frequently attack the competence and ideas of individuals who have prepared appropriately for discussion. The snide remarks made by the cynic only call attention to his inadequacy and lack of preparation. He frequently interrogates the better-prepared members under the guise of gaining full discussion when he is really directing the spotlight away from himself so that he will not be required to offer anything constructive.

Flight defenses are evident in people who choose to intellectualize about a subject rather than to deal with the real issue. Ancillary philosophizing about social and general behavior relative to the issue may be educational, but it is an evasion of the real goal of group discussion. Such individuals tend to generalize, never really coming to grips with the issue or their responsibility for producing an idea—lest they be subjected to the scrutiny, analysis, or ridicule of the group. They use such phrases as "people feel this way" or "they will react that way," when what they really mean is "I will do this or feel this way." By generalizing, they escape responsibility. Also, they frequently rationalize nonproductive behavior by substituting what they think are good reasons for the real motivation behind their lack of contribution. They project behavior and character traits unacceptable in themselves to other members of the group. The escapist may digress on an unrelated topic for fifteen minutes and conclude by saying, "Let's really get down to the issue," "I seem to be the only person dealing with the topic," or "Why doesn't someone else say something?"

A final flight from responsibility mentioned by Thorensen is withdrawal from the group, either intellectually or physically. Silence that is the result of withdrawal is not golden; it it not even dramatic—it is a bore.[20]

A discussion-group member may protect himself from deep involvement in conflict or confrontation by pairing with another individual to form

---

[20]P. Thorensen, "Defense Mechanisms in Groups," *The Nineteen Seventy-two Annual Handbook for Group Facilitators* (LaJolla, Calif.: University Associates), pp. 117–118.

a subgroup alliance that spreads the responsibility and makes the threat of contradiction less severe. Someone prone to do this frequently says, "Well, Joe and I feel this way," "Pete and I have talked about this previously," or "I know Ken feels the same way I do about this." This same person often comes to the aid of someone being attacked. He feels that the assistance that he provides will obligate the other person to come to his defense should the group turn on him. When the group finds that it is spending excessive time discussing the ideas of one individual, people might conclude that they are doing this to keep the focus away from themselves.

Defensive and offensive maneuvers within the group that evade the issue and obscure the goals, must be dealt with directly by the leader. When an individual understands that the motivation for his behavior is recognized by a leader whom he trusts, he is apt to risk experimenting with behavior that will improve his interpersonal skills.

Among the more destructive defenders against conflict, one can count the critic who attacks members of the group on a personal level rather than criticizing their ideas. This critic blames everyone else for failure to find a solution but offers none of his own. He may withhold valuable information or equipment from the group simply to prevent others from dealing with the subject—perhaps because he despises contention, or does not feel that he will make a significant contribution. This critic is more detrimental to progress than the individual who avoids conflict by reporting to outsiders what everybody in the group but himself has said, and then agreeing with his listener's evaluation of the situation.

The most baffling defensive mechanism is that of "gunny-sacking"—an individual repeatedly avoids dealing with a problem, disagreeing but silently storing up his resentment until it finally explodes when absolutely no one expects it.[21] After thoroughly chastising the group for past behavior, the "gunny-sacker" usually walks out of the room. Before inviting the "gunny-sacker" to the next meeting, the leader should counsel him about his nonproductive behavior.

CORRECTIVE MEASURES

Nonproductive activities and behavior must be discussed, preferably privately but sometimes telling the entire group that such behavior is undesirable and will not be tolerated. Should it persist, the obligation of the leader is to replace the destructive membership of the group. Do not disband the group; change the membership.

[21] Back and Wyden, *op. cit.*

Thomas Gordon suggests a method of handling nonproductive conflicts:

1. Identify and clearly define the conflict.
2. Generate a variety of solutions.
3. Evaluate the alternatives.
4. Reach consensus on the best alternatives.
5. Implement the selected alternatives.
6. Quickly ascertain if the implementation is working.[22]

Conflict is not satisfactorily resolved through vote, and it is not happily resolved when members agree in order to "get on to something else." Divergence of opinion is healthy. It is not a win-or-lose matter! Indeed all sides may win because the best solution may emerge from the difference's that were expressed. Conflict properly managed is productive. It is properly managed when it is reduced, resolved, or controlled so that it does not interfere with fruitful discussion. When the group has been given a clear definition of its goals and then uses conflict as a positive method of airing all points of view, conflict generates cohesiveness and is therefore desirable.

Order and Creativity

Although the desired end of discussion is agreement, disagreement furnishes the foundation. Disagreement must focus on issues; issues are points about which disagreement is crucial. Where disagreement is not crucial—when there are no issues—discussion is superfluous. Disagreement is stimulating; it maintains interest and forms a basis for eventual agreement.

The orderliness of a discussion will depend largely upon the preparation of the leader. An agenda with a preliminary analysis based on Dewey's "pattern of reflective thinking" or Alan Monroe's "motivated sequence" establishes a process by which solutions may be reached. The good leader is not so enamored of his agenda that he refuses to consider any variation because he recognizes fully that rigidity can stifle creativity. Dewey pointed out, "Each improvement in the idea leads to new observations that yield new facts or data and help the mind judge more accurately the relevance of the facts already at hand."[23] Such an observation suggests that it is sometimes very valuable to backtrack, perhaps arriving at a solution first and then reconstructing the reasons for that solution.

A good agenda is prepared and distributed well before the meeting so

[22]T. Gordon, *Parental Effectiveness Training* (New York: Peter W. Wyden, 1970), pp. 47–84.

[23]J. Dewey, *op. cit.,* p. 115.

that it may guide the group's preparation as well as their discussion. A well-prepared agenda helps the discussion leader keep the group on the topic. He is quick to acknowledge the worth of all ideas presented, even if some are irrelevant, but he quickly gets back to the issue at hand. He also furnishes transitions that move the group gracefully from one phase of discussion to the next so that it does not get bogged down on one point and fail to complete the agenda in the allotted time. Some staff meetings, however, have an "open agenda" whose purpose is simply to discuss problems of a general nature.

Recognize Contributions

The group leader is conscious of the contributions of all members. He encourages silent members to speak but is careful not to embarrass them with direct questions. He is alert to subtle nuances and nonverbal reactions that may indicate that an individual desires to speak but is reluctant to ask for attention. When the timid member does speak, a good leader is quick to praise his contribution.

A good leader also recognizes when he must squelch overly outspoken members who, by sheer strength of personality, can force the group to concentrate on a pet project or who introduce strongly emotional points or attitudes. Direct disagreement with this individual merely provokes argument and increases the volume rather than enlarges the content of discussion. If possible, with part of what the dominant individual has said, try to relate his comments to the specific purpose of the meeting, and then move directly back to the topic. It may be necessary to rephrase or restate completely the contentions made by this person so that they are more palatable to the entire group and let him know that you understood. The technique of rephrasing is important to avoid bruised egos and to protect such people from verbal attack by others.

Keep the Discussion Moving

As a leader, one does not have to remain neutral on every point of discussion. The leader's primary responsibility is to keep the discussion moving and to get all members of the group to express their views. Occasionally they will expect him to state his views. If called upon to do so, the leader should state frankly and concisely how he feels about an issue and stress that he is not forcing his point of view on the entire group but is flexible and open to change.

A good discussion leader is conscious of undesirable patterns that may emerge; for example, speaker A supports an issue and is immediately followed by speaker B, who takes the opposite side of the issue, or when speaker C speaks, he addresses his remarks exclusively to D and E rather than to the whole group. The leader can break such patterns by politely in-terrupting—either to give his opinion or to ask for the opinion of other members of the group.

When the leader discovers that discussion is thwarted because the group lacks sufficient information to proceed, he should terminate the discussion at that point, assign individuals to gather further information, and suggest that the discussion will continue at the next meeting. It is fruitless to continue discussing a subject without adequate information.

The leader is responsible for making internal summaries regarding specific issues and for concluding the discussion with a summary of what has been agreed upon, what has not, and the contributions made by each in-dividual to the discussion as a whole. He should also recommend and assign materials to be prepared for presentation at the next discussion, and he should make sure that he collects on these assignments. After the meeting has been concluded, the leader prepares and distributes the minutes and in-forms members of any additional responsibility they may have.

THE COMMITTEE

A committee was once described as "a group of the unfit, chosen by the un-willing to do the unwanted." Most discussion groups in healthy organiza-tions do not fit this description; they are selected, organized, and managed by a well-prepared, thoughtful, considerate, and energetic leader. Commit-tees are formed because smaller groups of specialists can proceed more effi-ciently than larger discussion groups and because specific research and ex-pertise are needed to provide information and recommendations for the larger group to make an intelligent selection.

Forms

There are two kinds of committees—standing committees and special, or *ad hoc,* committees. The standing committee is a permanent group whose name, character, and duties are stated by the by-laws of the organization. Members of the standing committee are usually appointed by the head of the organization. The special, or *ad hoc* committee, is a temporary group whose character and duties are assigned by the parent group or by the head of the organization. These committees go out of existence when they have performed a given task. Membership in special committees is either by ap-pointment or election.

The Chairperson

A committee chairperson may be appointed by the head of the organiza-tion or chosen from the membership of the committee. Research by specific members is pooled in discussion in order to assure that all possible solutions are presented for a given problem. Through informal discussions, the committee then chooses the best solution, which it reports to the parent body through its chairperson. The committee report may be accepted, adopted, or rejected by the parent body. A minority report may be submitted, and if so, it has the status of a substitute recommendation for the committee report.

Group discussion may take several forms. Eugene Bierbaum has described the forms that discussion may take, based upon the purpose, participants, and occasion.[24] These are the panel, roundtable, conference, symposium, dialogue, and forum. A *panel* is generally informal in procedure and held before an audience. It employs free interchange among participants rather than prepared formal speeches. The degree of informality may vary, and the purpose of the discussion may be problem solving, information sharing, information giving, or persuasion.

A semicircular seating arrangement for the panel is usually best because it enables the audience to see and hear with the least difficulty. Because there are usually no prepared speeches or no order of speaking, the panel discussion generally has a moderator whose function is to introduce the topic for discussion, attempt to keep the discussion orderly and organized, and conclude the discussion.

A *roundtable* functions largely like a panel but usually has no audience. It tends, therefore, to be more informal. Like the panel, it has a leader who encourages participants to engage in a free interchange of opinions and ideas. The term "roundtable" is also frequently applied to certain radio, television, and other discussions where informality is a chief characteristic.

The word "conference" sometimes designates any meeting, convention, or convocation. Thus, there may be a national or international conference of members of a profession, members of a trade union, or growers of red roses.

The word "conference" is frequently used to refer to the meetings of decision-making or policy-making groups, such as boards of directors or executive committees. It may apply to any discussion in business, industry, government, or other large organization.

A *symposium* is a discussion in which the members of the group each deliver a prepared speech. In most cases, the group consists of four to six members and has a leader or chairman (who may be one of the members of the group). By prearrangement, each member of the group has been assigned a particular aspect of the discussion topic for his special consideration. This kind of topic division may be chronological, spatial, problem-solving, topical, or any one of several other common methods of division of the subject.

[24]M. E. Bierbaum, 1976-77 President, American Institute of Parliamentarians, unpublished memorandum to the author, July 1977.

The time is usually divided equally among the participants, and each participant prepares and delivers a speech on his aspect of the topic. The chairperson's functions include introducing the topic, introducing the speakers, and connecting the speeches of the participants with brief remarks.

Physical arrangements resemble those of the usual speaker-audience setting. The speakers and the chairperson sit on a platform, or at least in front of an audience, and come forward in turn to speak. At the conclusion of the speeches, the chairperson summarizes the talks and leads a forum discussion if one has been planned. The symposium usually is more formal than a panel and better suited to informational rather than decision-making or persuasive purposes.

A *dialogue* is a two-member discussion "group." The interview situation is the most common example of the dialogue. One of the two participants asks the questions; the other primarily provides the answers. Typical examples of this kind of discussion are radio and television interviews. Johnny Carson, Merv Griffin, and Steve Allen furnish examples of public dialogues whose purpose is to entertain.

A *forum* is a general discussion in which the members of the audience have an opportunity to ask questions or make comments about the subject under discussion. A variety of stimuli might spark the forum. When the stimulus is a single speaker, we label the activity a "lecture-forum." But a film might also serve as the stimulus, as might any of the other types of discussion and conference considered here. Thus, we may refer to a film forum, a panel forum, a symposium forum, and so on.

In each case, in addition to the stimulus, it is common to have a chairperson who introduces the speaker, film, or other stimulus and who also moderates the forum period that follows.

When a group of experts on the discussion topic are engaged in discussion by non-expert representatives of the audience, the result is usually called a colloquy. In theory, at least, the representatives of the audience ask the questions, make the points, and say what every member of the audience wishes that he could say eloquently, forcefully, and directly. The purpose of the discussion is to learn. Although there are no set speeches and the flow of talk moves easily in a free give and take, the procedure is somewhat formal in that a chairperson moderates and experts sit on one side, the laymen on the other.

DISCUSSION CLASSIFIED ACCORDING TO PURPOSE

Problem Solving

Here the primary objective of the group is to solve a problem. The group begins with an unanswered question or problem and engages in careful discussion until an answer or solution is reached.

T-Group

This discussion method is designed to help people understand the process, functions, and structure of a group, the kinds of interpersonal relationships existing in groups, and the kinds of behavior that people manifest in group activities. The T-Group works best in a highly permissive, unstructured environment. Members of the group supply their own subject matter and way of dealing with it. One of the necessary features of the T-Group is immediate feedback. The group is expected to analyze itself and to assess what is happening to the group and to the behavior of individuals in the group. Strong, expert, professional guidance is necessary to prevent a breakdown because of personality conflicts. This exercise can be self-destructive if not controlled.

Role Playing

It can be very valuable to see others as they see themselves. It may be very useful in understanding human relationships and their implications in problem solving to attempt to get "inside" the feelings and thought processes of the people involved. Members of the group actually play the parts of the people involved. Some setting of the problem is needed, and some description of the positions and attitudes of the participants is required.

Brainstorming

A solution to a problem is sought. Members of the group are asked to state as many solutions or modifications of solutions as they can think of. A premium is placed on the number of solutions, and a record is kept of all suggestions. These are subsequently examined, analyzed, and tested, but this does not take place in the brainstorming session itself because it might hinder or inhibit the flow of suggested solutions.

Discussion methods may take many forms, but the specific purpose of discussion is to complete a given task. The success or failure of a discussion is determined when an honest evaluation is made by each participant and the leader, and by those who receive recommendations and solutions, and finally if and when productive action follows. Almost two hundred years ago, Hugh Blair succinctly stated the real value of group discussion: "Small are the advances which a single, unassisted individual can make toward perfecting any of his powers. What we call human reason is not the effort or ability of one, so much as it is the result of the reasoning of many, arising from lights mutually communicated, in consequence of discourse. . . ."[25]

[25]H. Blair, *Lectures on Rhetoric and Belles Letters* (London: T. Tegg, 1838), p. 1.

INTERVIEW
WITH A
PURPOSE

Chapter Ten

Because we so frequently participate in interviews, we tend to assume that we are proficient, that when we are informed and alert, interviewing skill comes naturally. Interviewing, however, is a unique form of communication with some solid techniques that are based on research and can be learned. Interviewing is not simply conversation, but rather a technique of discourse on a specific subject; it follows a preconceived pattern and is focused on achieving a specific purpose.

THE DYAD

Stuart and Cash define interviewing as "a process of dyadic communication with a predetermined and serious purpose, designed to interchange behavior, and usually involving the asking and answering of questions."[1] The dyad is a form of interpersonal communication between two individuals in which the roles of speaker and listener are constantly exchanged, based upon the verbal and nonverbal signaling during the conversation. Such intimate communication can provoke emotional reactions; it involves risk taking and self-disclosure, and these often induce stress. To

[1]C. Stuart and W. Cash, *Interviewing Principles and Practices* (Dubuque, Iowa: William C. Brown, 1974), p. 4.

minimize the undesirable aspect of the dyad, both parties must consciously or unconsciously agree that exchanges will be in socially acceptable form.

To assure the sociability of the interview situation, the interviewer should be prepared with purposeful questions that are relevant to the subject and appropriately chosen to elicit the best information available from the interviewee. Answers to previously prepared questions form the basis for progress of the interview toward its goal. The interviewer cannot in every instance predict the answer to his questions, but careful analysis of the situation, individual, subject matter, and ultimate goal will help him to anticipate a response.

There are four tenets that I have used as guides during the many years I have conducted interviews—courtesy, concern, control, and common sense.

Courtesy

Courtesy directly affects the perception of the interviewee. When someone is rudely treated by a secretary, kept waiting past the appointment time, interrupted during the interview by telephone conversations or by an interviewer who wishes to discourse about something entirely unrelated to the situation, and finds the interview terminated before he feels that he has had an opportunity to complete his presentation, he is apt to conclude that the interview was unsuccessful and not want to subject himself to a repetition of such treatment. An interviewee *feels* better when he is greeted at the door by an interviewer who is appropriately dressed for the occasion and ushers him into the room and when he feels that he has the full attention of the interviewer during their conversation.

The courteous manager begins and concludes the interview on time. He communicates pleasure in having experienced the interviewee's presence by walking him to the office door, shaking hands, and bidding him a friendly farewell. In these concluding remarks, much good will can be established by commenting on matters really unrelated to the subject but rather to the individual. Although "small talk" is inappropriate during the actual business of the interview, the concluding walk from the office is a good opportunity for friendly and spirit-lifting exchanges, and it will establish a common ground that assures further open communication should the manager desire it. Courteous treatment is an obvious and overt signal that an individual is concerned about the happiness and welfare of another.

Concern

Concern is also communicated when the manager has previously prepared by learning all he can about the individual with whom he will speak. The manager may gain information from a dossier or resume compiled by the interviewee and from information gathered by asking discreet questions of acquaintances, previous employers, or employees. No matter how the manager gets the information, the fact that he has it allows him to frame questions and supply answers that indicate clearly that he has bothered to find out about the individual and that he is interested in the individual and deeply concerned with solving a problem, solidifying a situation, or providing an evaluation.

The concerned interviewer expresses concern when he really listens to the individual before he reacts, evaluates, or comments in response to his questions. He expresses his concern when he defines the terms and conditions of the interview so that purpose and procedure are clearly understood. He makes an individual feel that he has participated in and contributed to the conclusions of the interview. He is careful not to dent the respondent's self-image by drawing hasty conclusions. He solicits the interviewee's points of view and ascertains his values and attitudes about social and economic conditions without giving his own judgment as to the worth of these beliefs.

He may offer advice about the kind of behavior that has been most productive in the organization and the kind that has not. He recognizes, through the verbal response to questions and the nuances of nonverbal signals when tension is arising and minimizes it by changing his questioning technique or perhaps by injecting a touch of humor into the conversation. Concern is most readily apparent when the interviewee feels that he has the undivided attention of a well-prepared and sensitive interviewer and when the interview has been structured in such a way as to lead to some meaningful end.

Control

Structure and purpose form the foundation for control. The properly prepared interviewer starts with a preconceived purpose and then eliminates all extraneous materials so that he may focus upon content. He considers the situation and the individual and adapts his plan to both. Although a large portion of the interview may be extemporaneous, a solid plan will leave little to chance. One may select Dewey's model for "reflective thinking" as a pattern of organization.[2] In this model, Dewey contends that (1) the problem is recognized, (2) the problem is defined, (3) solutions are suggested, (4) solutions are examined and compared, and (5) the best solution is chosen and verified. This kind of orderly thought process provides a basis for discussion that is both flexible enough for full discourse and yet pointed toward an ultimate conclusion. Dewey's model also insures an opportunity for full participation by both individuals in the interview situation but imposes a format that is logical, reasonable, and easy to follow. At the conclu-

[2]J. Dewey, *How We Think* (Boston: D. C. Heath, 1910), p. 107.

sion of the interview, the interviewer should summarize what has been agreed upon and what has not and then emphasize the action that will be taken as a result of the discussion.

Besides controling the interview through a preconceived plan, one can affect certain Machiavellian behavior that asserts authority. The interviewer who is concerned about his authority may place himself in front of a large window or impressive picture, sit in an impressive chair behind a large desk and assign a smaller chair, directly across from him, to the other person, or humble himself by performing a personal service. Years ago an administrator with whom I worked used to remove a shoebrush from his desk and proceed to shine the interviewee's shoes while providing "advice and counsel." Many of my colleagues agreed that it was very difficult to argue with a man who was shining one's shoes. The problem with these and other contrived gimmicks is that when they are detected, they frequently produce defensiveness.

The intention of the interview may be to induce a change of behavior, seek information or convey it, or solve a corporate or individual problem. No matter what form the interview takes, the interviewer should clearly be in control of the situation. Control ensues when preparation is evident.

Common Sense

Control of an interview is also influenced by one's ability to use common sense. The interviewer should base his questions on his perceptions of the other individual and that person's state of mind, recognizing that he may be nervous, anxious, or confused or distraught about the circumstances that have caused the interview to take place. To ease the tension, the interviewer may simply repeat comments made by the interviewee. This technique of "permissive listening" allows the individual to say whatever he likes without fear of blame and the danger of misdirected approval. Frequently, when someone hears what he has said repeated, the statement takes on a different meaning or a different connotation that relieves the speaker from the previously hidden meaning, feeling, or attitude that he attached to it.

The interviewer who is humble, silent, and attentive will learn much because permissive listening encourages free and full discussion that can be extremely beneficial. It allows both interviewer and interviewee to identify the problem and formulate solutions to it.

Ordinarily it is inadvisable to interrupt an individual in midsentence. Interrupting can be advantageous if used selectively, however, to convey to certain individuals that the listener is "really with them." Unfortunately it conveys most often the impression that the listener does not really care what the first speaker is saying and that the listener wants to get on with the conversation "to something more important."

Like concern, common sense based on perception will prevent an interviewer from denting someone else's self-image. The interviewer must make every effort to be sensitive to the other person's personality and needs; he can demonstrate this sensitivity by his choice of language, timing of questions, willingness to listen without interrupting or passing judgment, and appropriate preparation.

Should a problem be technically or psychologically beyond the expertise of the interviewer, he should refer the interviewee to someone else— sometimes, depending on the situation, an expert in the area or a professional counselor. The good counseling interviewer has a list of available experts for ready referral. Bluffing through a situation that one is incompetent to handle can be extremely detrimental to the organization and is potentially harmful to the person being counseled.

The sensible interviewer understands that most people who come to his office are tense because they do not know what to expect—including what the outcome of the conversation will be. They have either been summoned or have come of their own volition to get something that they need, want, expect, or dread. The thoughtful interviewer attempts to minimize their anxiety through his own behavior. He knows when to probe further and when to be silent. He recognizes when discussion has ceased to be fruitful and should be terminated, and he closes the conversation in such a way as to keep the channels of communication open for further discourse.

SPECIAL CONSIDERATIONS

Although interviews are much more informal than other forms of public address, they are nevertheless more structured than conversation. Stuart and Cash believe that participation in an interview should follow a ratio of seventy percent to thirty percent, with the interviewee doing most of the talking.[3] When the interviewer talks more than thirty percent of the time, he is giving a speech to an audience of one and is wasting both his and the interviewee's time. Any manager who cannot ascertain an individual's qualifications for employment in a one-hour interview or who spends two or three hours hearing an employee complaint is probably spending more time talking than listening. A manager can determine whether he has this fault if, in his next interview, he discreetly keeps a stopwatch in his hand and starts and stops it each time he speaks; he can then subtract his total speaking time from the time taken to complete the interview. That timing device can be very revealing!

Because interviews are more intimate, they are more valuable than other forms of communication for discovering thoughts, beliefs, feelings, and attitudes, and sometimes these revelations become clear only through

[3]Stuart and Cash, *op. cit.,* p. 13.

planned digressions from the main point. Digression is not usually planned in other forms of communication. The interviewer must be extremely well-prepared because the interview situation allows interruption at any time for clarification or support of a point. Because of the intimate nature of the interview situation, participants risk much more exposure than in any other communication situation. The interviewer must be clever at extemporaneous reply to inquiry and should never communicate shock or anger; to do so is to lose control and permit an undesirable digression.[4]

Replies in interviews take three forms—confirmation, denial, or modification and adjustment. Confirmation and denial are quickly expressed both verbally and nonverbally, but modification requires the use of carefully chosen language and a clear focus upon form and goals.

The Directive Interview

Interviews take two basic forms; they are either directive or nondirective. In the directive interview, the interviewer convenes the session, establishes the purpose, and controls the pacing of the conversation. Directive interviews may be both information-giving and information-gathering; the employment interview is a typical example. Directive interviews are easy to control; the techniques are simple to learn, and the interviews generally take little time.

Some of the things that make the directive interview advantageous, however, are also detrimental. The form is inflexible, and the interviewer does not have a wide range of techniques to investigate a variety of subjects.

The Nondirective Interview

The nondirective interview, by design, allows the interviewee to suggest the purpose, pace, and subject of the interview. "Design" is the key word in the above sentence; for although it may seem to the interviewee that he is furnishing all the information and solving all the problems, the interviewer structures his questions in such a way as to motivate an introspective, personal approach to offering solutions. The interviewee, in essence, furnishes answers to his own problem based upon his answers to questions presented by the interviewer and the interviewer's feedback to his responses.

The nondirective interview is more flexible and thus provides more opportunity for dealing with a wider range of subjects; it also allows more in-depth study of personal or organizational problems. It requires more time than the directive interview, and it requires a much more sensitive and well-trained interviewer for success.

[4]A. Benjamin, *The Helping Interview* (Boston: Houghton Mifflin, 1969), pp. 34–56.

QUALITIES OF A GOOD INTERVIEWER

Experience as an interviewer is not necessarily related to the quality of the interview unless the interviewer knows what he is doing. He must understand clearly that he can terminate a conversation at any time—but that the impressions caused by interaction continued long after the meeting. He is aware of the necessity to define goals and terms clearly and of the ways in which emphasis on words and phrases changes meaning and modifies replies to his questions.

The experienced interviewer has trained himself to be very perceptive regarding the programming of the interviewee and of himself. Programming is the automatic behavior we exhibit as a result of our prejudice, blindspots, or simply our environment and training. He knows that this programming determines how others respond to specific "trigger" words and subjects; he is therefore selective in his language choice and is astute when he chooses subjects for discussion. He knows when to be silent.

The experienced interviewer never assumes that he is fully understood because he knows that many people in subordinate or threatened positions are reluctant to admit that they do not understand; therefore, he confirms by further questions or rephrases his response in order to validate comprehension. He is aware of encoding—the process by which people put together all components of a message, verbal and nonverbal, in order to arrive at meaning.[5]

The experienced interviewer is a good listener. He knows that the length of his questions influences the length of the responses; individuals tend to give lengthy responses to lengthy questions. He knows that females behave differently from males in an interview situation; they engage in more eye contact and display less anxiety when interviewed by a male. Female behavior tends to be somewhat more modified by the appearance of the interviewer and less by his use of language. Women tend to view a man who is neat and well-dressed as informed and authoritative and a man who is poorly dressed or sloppy as someone who "doesn't know any better."[6]

The experienced interviewer has learned that an atmosphere of friendliness and warmth minimizes anxiety. He has carefully arranged the conditions leading up to the interview and conducts business in a room with furnishings that are conducive to creating an appropriate atmosphere. Tension tends to disrupt the normal rhythms of an individual and may cause the interviewee to increase rapidly his rate of speech, perhaps to stammer or fall into nonproductive silence. The experienced interviewer has become very conscious of the immediate, the first, response to his questions. Should the

[5]D. E. Broadbent, *Perceptions in Communication* (New York: Pergamon Press, 1958).
[6]C. Stuart and W. Cash, *op. cit.,* pp. 107–108.

interviewee perceive any negative verbal or nonverbal attitude or behavior, his response frequently will be slow and brief—thus limiting the opportunity for more extensive, more probing questions.

Enlightenment

The goal for both participants in an interview should be enlightenment, which may take the form of counseling, giving and sharing of information, or simply providing a new experience. It is the responsibility of the experienced interviewer to conduct himself so that the greatest enlightenment will be realized. Enlightenment proceeds from a warm and friendly atmosphere; it is stimulated by an informed, interested, experienced interviewer who asks the correct question in an appropriate sequence. His questions may be open-ended, which allows freedom for broad, general responses, or when direct information and specific facts are required, he may choose closed questions.

Open-Ended Questions

Open-ended questions place the full responsibility for reply upon the interviewee; they connote an interest in him personally and a confidence in his ability to answer clearly, accurately, and in whatever detail he selects. Many interviews start with open-ended questions because the freedom that they allow poses only minor threats to the individual. He may volunteer as much or as little information as he chooses. Such questions allow him to reveal what he thinks is important and, as a consequence, may provide information not possible to obtain through closed questions. Open-ended questions have the advantage of providing information that the skilled interviewer may probe for deeper meaning.

A disadvantage of the open-ended question is that, when it is not skillfully framed, it may allow inordinate time for the response, thus using all the time allotted for the interview but not providing all the information desired by the interviewer. The inexperienced interviewer will also have some difficulty in quantifying the answers to open-ended questions; certainly he will have difficulty when comparing different people's responses to the same open-ended question. Open-ended questions may be completely unrestricted ("Tell me about yourself") or somewhat restricted ("Describe your responsibility in the position you presently occupy" or "What really seem to be the problems in your organizational unit?").

Closed Questions

Because closed questions are restrictive, they limit the possible answers. Closed questions may ask for specific information—"What salary do you require?"—or they may ask the individual to select several possible answers—for example, "Is your principal strength in accounting, personnel, management, or research?" Closed questions may require the interviewee to rank items in order of preference or worth. When specific information is required, the interviewer may phrase questions which can be answered yes or no—such as "Are you married?" "Have you completed your degree?" "Would you be willing to relocate?"[7]

Closed questions permit the interviewer to carefully control the interview and to get information quickly. The closed question requires a less sensitive, less skillful interviewer; answers are also much easier to tabulate. A closed question prevents an interviewee from volunteering information; a closed question, mischosen, may polarize interviewee and interviewer and thus set up a barrier that adversely affects the remainder of the interview. Such questions also allow an interviewee to supply an answer without really understanding the question or its intent. Both open-ended and closed questions should be selectively employed in the interview in order to elicit the type of information desired.

Secondary Questions

Primary questions introduce topics, and secondary questions elicit further information. Kahn and Cannell suggest that when the interviewer feels that he has not received a complete answer, he may remain silent for a moment—hoping that the pause will encourage the respondent to continue. Or he may employ such phrases as "Go on," "Tell me more," or "What happened next?" He might also say, "Would you elaborate on that point?" "Then what did you do?" or "Why did you react that way?" Should the interviewee provide a vague generality, the interviewer might say, "I'm not sure I fully understand" or "Would you define that for me?" He may use a "reflective probe" in order to double check his interpretation, saying, "Then you really do think Phil is honest?" or "By supervision—you truly *do* mean snooping?" "Did you actually *hear* John say that?"[8]

Reflective Probes

Reflective probes should be expressed in a way that indicates a desire for understanding and not disbelief. When an answer suggests a negative feeling or attitude, the interviewer might ask, "What do you suppose caused you to feel that way?" or "Who do you think is really responsible for this situation?"

Occasionally, an interviewee does not answer a question because he thinks it is irrelevant, because he does not have the information or believes

[7]P. B. Sheatsley, "Closed Questions Are Sometimes More Valid than Open End," *Public Opinion Quarterly,* 22 (1948): 12.
[8]R. L. Kahn and C. F. Cannell, *The Dynamics of Interviewing* (New York: John Wiley and Sons, 1964), pp. 217-220.

that his answer might prejudice the interviewer against him. If this does occur, consider restating or rephrasing the question, but if no answer is forthcoming, don't pursue the matter further.

When the interviewer suspects deliberate inaccuracy in answer to a question, he might take one of two tacks: (1) He might consider supplying the correct information by saying "You mean ___, don't you?" (2) He might say, "Did I hear you say (the inaccurate information)?" or "Did I hear you say (the correct information)?" In case the interviewer suspects that qualifying words or phrases have been omitted from quotations, he might ask "Did ___ say 'probably' or 'could be' or 'occasionally'?" When the interviewer discovers or suspects that he has been given an unintentionally inaccurate answer, he might use a reflective probe, supplying the correct information; for example, "You've been here four years rather than three, haven't you?" or "Let's stop and think about that a moment because I recall that it's been less than three years since you were promoted." The interviewer must decide whether it's better to let the inaccuracy stand or to correct the inaccuracy but at the risk of questioning the integrity of the interviewee.

The Need to Explain

When an interviewee tells you that he cannot answer one of your questions, explain to him why you requested the information and how it will be used, and consider rephrasing the question or describing the kind of answer or information that you thought he might give. Should these techniques fail to elicit an appropriate answer, do not pursue the matter. Failure to move on to another point will only increase the interviewee's anxiety and may promote hostility.

Summary Questions

Summary or mirror questions are used for clarification. They are the result of a series of questions and answers that lead to an overall picture of a situation or point of view. For example, an interviewer might say, "If I understand you correctly, you plan to complete the management training course, assist Robinson in his research project, and furnish leadership in the apprentice program—plus carry on with your regularly assigned responsibilities?" The mirror question assures that the interviewer fully understands the answers that he has received and also has the advantage of clearly pointing out to the interviewee ancillary conditions and impressions that may consequently furnish the foundation for successful completion of the conversation. This technique leads to clear understanding and affirmative action toward a determined goal.[9]

[9]*Ibid.,* pp. 210–213.

Secondary questions well phrased, appropriate to the context, and properly emphasized for intended meaning give the impression that the interviewer is genuinely interested in the answer and in the person giving it; thus, they encourage further response.

Leading and "Loaded" Questions

Leading or "loaded" questions often do not reveal very much except the interviewer's prejudice. Questions like "You are a hard worker, aren't you?" "Do you take directions well?" and "How do you feel about the restrictions imposed by union shops?" elicit only answers that the interviewee feels confident the interviewer desires.

Leading or loaded questions may be useful in appraisal or employment interviews when the goal is to learn how the interviewee responds under stress or to ascertain his susceptibility to authoritative influence. Because the psychological ramifications of the "stress interview" are so severe, it should only be conducted, and its results interpreted, by a trained expert.

ORGANIZATION

The format for questions may be in an inductive order, which proceeds from the specific to the general, or in a deductive order—which proceeds from the general to the specific.

Induction

A sequence of questions patterned on inductive reasoning starts with closed questions and gradually proceeds to broad open-ended ones. The inductive method of questioning is particularly valuable when it is desirable to elicit specific information in order to draw general conclusions. The interviewee may not want to talk about unpleasant situations, may not totally grasp a situation, or may need time to gather his thoughts before he is able to express them completely. Closed questions permit the interviewee to give answers that may lead to the development of broader concepts. These brief answers often serve as "pump primers" for extended discussion.

Deduction

Conversely, a pattern of questioning based upon deduction begins with open-ended questions that are broad and general in nature. They can best be used when the interviewer perceives that the interviewee is generally relaxed and confident. The open-ended question gives the interviewee an opportunity to speak about something without committing himself to one particular idea or one point of view, and so avoiding the polarization that can occur when one is asked a specific question about a particular emotional or traumatic situation. The open-ended question furnishes the basis for a later response of a more specific nature and may even provide information that makes additional questions unnecessary.

Quintamensional Sequence

The quintamensional sequence of questions used by the Gallup Poll and others employs a five-step approach which this example by Stuart and Cash illustrates:

1. Awareness ("Tell me what you know about management consulting.")
2. Uninfluenced Attitudes ("What, if any, are the contributions made to organizations by consultants?")
3. Specific Attitudes ("Do you approve or disapprove of consulting?")
4. Reason Why ("Why do you feel that way?")
5. Intensity of Attitude ("How strongly do you feel about this?—strongly very strongly, not something you will ever change your mind on?")[10]

This form of questioning quickly provides information about the attitudes and intensity of feeling regarding a specific situation.

Gathering Opinion

A further method of inquiry involves a sequence of similar questions that allow little probing and depend for their effectiveness upon the primary answer. These questions may be used to gather opinions about people, places, conditions, and procedures. The interviewer may ask an individual to rate John, Joe, Jack, and Phil in terms of their supervisory capability or to decide whether the meeting should be in Lake Placid, Philadelphia, Syracuse, or Columbus. He might ask if the meeting should be a symposium, panel, colloquia, or roundtable. This kind of questioning generally does not ask why but restricts itself to opinions about who, what, where, how, and when.

The kinds of questions asked and their sequence depend upon the individual being interviewed, the context of the interview, and the goal. All forms of questions and all techniques of ordering questions are appropriate and may be effective for gaining specific information.

[10]Stuart and Cash, *op. cit.*, p. 65. Reprinted with special permission of William C. Brown Publishers.

FORMS ACCORDING TO PURPOSE

Interviews may be classified according to purpose. The information-giving interview provides an opportunity for orientation, general instruction, and job-related training. The information-gathering interview may be used by a manager when he wishes to get opinions from the people in his department, learn why an individual is leaving his organization, or discover feelings or attitudes that are causing nonproductive behavior. He may simply wish to find out what someone wants or needs.

The selection interview is another form of information gathering used frequently for screening and hiring new employees and for reassigning of individuals within the organization. The selection interview helps to validate previously known information so that the best employment decision may be made.

The most difficult interviews that management has to conduct are those that involve employee behavior—evaluation, appraisal, termination, correction, and discipline. These interviews are conducted at the insistence of the interviewer and pose a threat to the interviewee. Closely related to this type of interview is the one in which the interviewer receives complaints, minor grievances, or specialized or personal questions. The problem-solving interview involves organizational problems and change and follows the same pattern and has the same purpose as group discussion.

The persuasive interview is one in which the manager attempts to change someone's mind, to reaffirm a belief, to get others to accept a proposition or plan, or to persuade someone to buy his product or services. Persuasive techniques mentioned in the section on public speaking are applicable; they simply must be adapted to a one-to-one situation.

Interviews provide an opportunity to judge other people's communication skills and to discover attitudes and beliefs. Because the interviewer can, through his interpretation of questions and answers, guide the response of the interviewee, he is likely to get a more detailed and more accurate feedback than in any other form of communication. The interviewer who has firm control, based upon preparation and perception, can better evaluate and validate the information he receives by observing the interviewee's nonverbal reactions. Although an interview does not provide the only criteria regarding the character or competence of an individual, it is a reliable tool for decision-making when practiced by an expert.

INFORMATION GATHERING

The information-gathering interview intends to collect accurate and complete information in the shortest possible time. To accomplish this task, the interviewer must decide what information he needs, why he needs it, how the information is going to be used once he has it, and then who can supply that information. He carefully limits the subject of his inquiry and assiduously researches the topic in order to establish his credibility with the interviewee. The interviewer's previous research and preparation should enable him to structure a sequence of questions absolutely relevant to the topic and ones that the interviewee is capable of and agreeable to answering. Since the interviewer chooses the subject for the information-gathering interview, he also has the option of selecting the most desirable participants.

Opening Comments

When opening the information-gathering interview, the first step should be to establish trust and good will and to reach common ground by orienting the interviewee to the purpose of the inquiry. He will want to know what is expected of him, how the information he provides will be used, and perhaps how long the interview will last. It is better not to begin the interview with a question but rather with the reason for the interview, a summary of the problem, a request for assistance, a reference to someone who has indicated that the interviewee might have the information needed, or a statement about why the interviewer is asking this specific individual for information.

First Question

The opening question in the body of the interview furnishes a transition from the amenities of introduction to the actual purpose of the interview. It should be a question that is easy to answer so as to assure the respondent of his ability to participate successfully and thereby satisfy the previously stated purpose.

Major Questions

Informational interviewing should utilize both open-ended and closed questions, structured in such a way as to provide opportunity for probing into answers and enough flexibility to adapt to different responses. Questions must not be so loosely organized that they permit rambling answers that are time-consuming and difficult to evaluate. The well-prepared interviewer has developed a series of basic questions, followed by a variety of possible probes. When he has answers to each of his major questions and has amplified and clarified those answers through appropriate secondary questions, he can obtain valid information within the constraints of time allotted for the interview.

Clarity and Propriety

All questions should be relevant to the purpose of the interview. Should the interviewer perceive that there is some reluctance to answer a question, he should explain why this information is needed and how it is related to the business of the interview. One should not ask questions when he knows that the respondent does not have the information. The respondent may fake the information or be embarrassed by his inadequacy to answer. In either case, nothing is accomplished and anxiety may result in communication breakdown.

Unless used for a very specific purpose by a skilled interviewer, informational questions that infringe on social or psychological propriety should not be asked.[11] If such questions do seem necessary, never ask them early in the interview but only after appropriate and reasonable requests for information have established a reassuring sense of empathy and trust. A business interview is not the occasion to satisfy puerile curiosity.

When the interviewer is not of the same race, age, sex, or nationality as the interviewee, special problems may arise. The interviewer may be very skilled, but simply because certain of his physical characteristics differ from those of the interviewee, the latter may decide that the interviewer is incapable of understanding or sympathy. In that case, consider who in the organization is most likely to elicit the most accurate response in a given interview and assign that person to conduct it.

Note Taking

Occasionally it is desirable to record portions or perhaps all of an interview so that the content may be reviewed and answers from a number of people compared and contrasted. Personally, I advise against tape-recording interviews. A tape recorder sometimes malfunctions, leaving the interviewer with only his memory, but the most serious problem is the psychological stress caused by the interviewee's knowledge that what he says and how he says it (his language, his grammar, his vocal qualities) are being indelibly recorded for future scrutiny. This alone may create an insurmountable barrier to free and open responses.

If you want to take notes, ask the interviewee whether that bothers him. If it does, don't do it! Should he give you permission to take notes, try to do it without breaking eye contact. Take notes when the interviewee looks away for a moment. Avoid giving him cues about what you feel is important by recording his answers immediately after he provides them; don't start to write his answer to one question until he is well into answering

[11]Kahn and Cannell, *op. cit.,* pp. 123–126.

another. To assure that your notes are accurate, at the end of the interview read back to the interviewee enough of them to confirm mutual understanding. As soon as the interview is completed, synthesize the notes to secure a unified written impression of what was said. Your notes may also include impressions of *how* a person reacted to a question as well as his answer. These recorded impressions help an interviewer form a final impression about the success of the interview, analyze the validity of the questions used, structure future interviews, and perfect interviewing technique.

The informational interview should be carefully tailored to each situation, pointed to achieving a specific purpose, and addressed to the availability, capability, and personality of the interviewee.

Closing Comments

The conclusion for the information-gathering interview should be brief; thank the interviewee for his participation, and ask whether he has any questions about how and when the information that he provided will be used.

EMPLOYMENT INTERVIEW

The employment interview offers an opportunity to supplement written material in support of a candidate. Calvin Downs concludes that the employment interview permits the individual to answer thoroughly questions he may have only alluded to in written form. The face-to-face encounter allows the interviewer to form perceptions about the interviewee's poise, behavior, appearance, and how he reacts in one-to-one communication situations.[12] It also affords an opportunity to exchange information and to eliminate ambiguities that may have appeared in either the job description or the candidate's credentials.

Criteria for Evaluation

Because to the interviewee, the interviewer represents and personalizes his organization, his behavior directly influences the interviewee's attitudes and opinions about the organization. Robert Martin, in an effort to develop criteria for evaluating interviewees, presented to a group of supervisors a list of fifty items used to evaluate potential employees.[13] The most relevant criteria that emerged were: general intelligence, ability to communicate,

[12]C. W. Downs, "What Does the Selection Interview Accomplish?" *Personnel Administration* (1969): 8–14.
[13]R. A. Martin, "Toward More Productive Interviewing," *Personnel Journal,* 50 (1971): 359–364.

maturely directed energy, ambition, specific professional competence, integrity, attitude, personality, creativity, growth potential, compatibility, experience, sincerity, and capability for the specific job. The problem, of course, is that these qualities are extremely difficult to ascertain by all but the most skillful interviewer. Observation of an employee's performance is perhaps the most reliable method of validating information gained in the employment interview.

The interviewer receives specific information about the employee's age, training, and previous positions that allows him to make certain assumptions about the individual's ability. During the actual interview, these assumptions may be reinforced by responses that indicate defensiveness, nervousness, spontaneity, cooperation, and a variety of other attitudes and behavior. The astute interviewer is conscious that respondents may avoid certain issues or questions, omit information, or readily grasp the significance of questions that communicate values, strengths, fears, and motives in their behavior. Facts, observations, and inferences then furnish the foundation for the judgments that we make about an individual's ability successfully to fill a specific job. Note, however, that the effectiveness of the interview is much more dependent upon the interviewer's ability to collect and evaluate relevant information than upon the qualifications of the potential employee!

Because interviewers tend to develop their own stereotypes about what is a good candidate, their conclusions should be checked with a follow-up of employee's performance. When performance does not consistently agree with the interviewer's conclusions about potential, the prudent and efficient organization should choose someone else to conduct employment interviews.

Opening Comments

When beginning the employment interview, start with a friendly, warm greeting and then proceed directly into a question that is easy to answer. Some interviewers like to start with idle chatter, but this can sometimes confuse the respondent and is a waste of time. Should the interviewer feel the need for extended "ice breaking," in order to establish rapport, such conversation should be relevant to the individual and to the subject. He knows who he is, what his qualifications are, and why he is there, so presumably he will be more relaxed when answering questions about these subjects.

Interviewers might also consider opening the employment interview with a brief description of the company and the potential for contribution and growth. Such statements provide an opportunity for the candidate to make certain observations about his desires, goals, and ambitions. Should the interviewer sense unusual tension, he may suggest shifting the interview to another location—perhaps the cafeteria—or conducting the interview while the two individuals stroll about the campus or company grounds. A shift of scenery is often relaxing to both participants. The interviewer should never do or say anything that directly communicates to the interviewee that he recognizes that the latter is nervous or tense. This will only increase the applicant's anxiety.

Effective Techniques

Stuart and Cash have set forth some basic guidelines for clear and effective questioning in an employment interview: "(1) make all questions audible; do not mumble, (2) avoid memorizing the scheduled questions; memorization makes questions sound too mechanical, (3) do not waste time questioning about information you already have or do not need, (4) avoid asking questions already answered on the resume or application form, (5) be aware of what you are communicating non-verbally by tone of voice, eye movement, or shifting in your seat, (6) avoid evaluative responses to answers, (7) do not employ a 'machine gun' approach to questioning; give the applicant time to answer each question even if a few seconds' pause seems like hours, (8) use loaded or leading questions only for a definite and predetermined purpose, (9) use trick questions only when absolutely necessary; the interview is not a contest between interviewer and interviewee, (10) use speculative questions with the understanding that you will get speculative answers. For example, 'Where do you hope to be professionally in ten years?' (11) avoid questions that can be answered 'yes' or 'no,' (12) avoid questions that might violate fair employment practices legislation. For example: 'What is your native language?' 'What is your religious preference?' 'Name all clubs and organizations you belong to.' (13) give the applicant an opportunity to ask questions."[14]

Occasionally it is desirable during an employment interview to gather sensitive information regarding arrest records, marital status, home life or health. The interviewer should tell the applicant why he wants the information and ask for it directly. Should the information not be provided or should the interviewer notice equivocation, he has the choice of probing further or moving on to another subject and gathering the necessary information from other sources.

Closing Comments

The closing of the employment interview should be neutral. No promises or commitments should be made, and no negative opinion about the

[14]C. Stuart and W. Cash, *op. cit.,* pp. 151–152. Reprinted with special permission—William C. Brown Publishers.

individual's qualifications or his potential for being hired should be expressed. The interviewee should be informed of the next step in the process and given the name and address of someone with whom he can correspond. He should be encouraged to write or call should he have further questions or need clarification regarding the status of his candidacy. When an exact date on which the position will be filled is known, provide it.

Follow Up

Follow-up telephone calls to individuals suggested as references by the candidate, and perhaps to some who have not been suggested, are conducted by the astute interviewer in order to confirm assumptions he has made about the qualifications of the candidate. These telephone calls have the same status as confidential recommendations and are another way to check an applicant's qualifications.

All follow-up letters informing candidates of their status should be individually typed and signed. When the successful candidate starts work, all personal papers should be returned to the unsuccessful applicants. On occasion, an organization may wish to keep a file of the unsuccessful applicants as a pool for further consideration; if this is done, the applicants should be notified. Should one demur, return his papers; he is not interested in your organization.

APPRAISAL INTERVIEW

The very nature of the appraisal interview, with its requirements for evaluation and direction, makes it emotionally charged and consequently a potential threat to both interviewer and interviewee. The interviewer should, of course, have good documentation from a variety of sources to validate his impression of competence or incompetence, but his interpretation of these materials is also being influenced by his own attitudes, values, experience, and perceptions. The interviewee's anxiety is heightened in the appraisal situation because his subordinate position usually prevents him from overtly expressing evaluative opinions about the interviewer or the organization. Should he become angry, he often will suppress it, choosing to accept the evaluation or perhaps demurring only slightly and suggesting a different interpretation more favorable to himself. To minimize defensiveness and soften the threat, the appraisal interview should be conducted in an extremely supportive style, characterized by strong indications of empathy and thoughtful suggestions for alternative, satisfactory behavior.

Minimizing Negativeness

Kindall and Gatza have suggested methods of minimizing negativeness identified with appraisal interviews.[15] Their evaluation procedure begins with a clear agreement regarding the job description—what the person is paid to do and for what he is accountable. The job description provides parameters that the interviewee and the supervisor can use to help them agree upon performance targets. A worker may present or discuss plans with his supervisor for reaching these targets, and the supervisor may establish checkpoints for measuring the subordinate's progress. The appraisal interview culminates with a decision about the worker's success in achieving established goals. Many organizations prefer this kind of evaluation because it creates the impression that all employees are fully informed of the basis for their evaluation and are made aware of the target dates for achieving results.

Modifying Behavior

The appraisal interview has several purposes—to communicate evaluation, to improve growth and development of personnel, and to provide an outlet for defensive feelings that may be the cause of nonproductiveness. The interviewer who intends to influence someone to modify his behavior uses a variety of persuasive techniques. The assumption is that the employee is capable but has not seen the value of performing in the way that the organization expects. The manager assumes that a worker will understand the necessity for change and appreciate the suggestions made. This type of appraisal interview is most effective when the interviewer has a highly regarded reputation (based upon his own achievements) within the organization. He appeals to the employee's professional pride and other values to motivate improvement.[16]

A second approach is one in which the interviewer presents an evaluation and then asks how and why the respondent feels as he does about that evaluation. This interviewer must be an extremely good listener because the success of the interview depends upon the secondary questions that he poses in response to the subordinate's expressed feelings. The assumption in this kind of interview is that when an individual realizes that his behavior is not desirable, he will change it. Two-way communication is encouraged, it may modify the evaluation and enhance the worker's favorable attitude toward the interviewer and the organization.

[15]A. F. Kindall and J. Gatza, "Positive Program of Performance Appraisal," *Harvard Business Review,* 41 (1963): 1.
[16]*Ibid.,* pp. 4–5.

Problem Solving

The problem-solving evaluation assumes that discussion of the problem will lead to improvement. This kind of interview also requires two-way communication and puts increased responsibility on the subordinate for providing answers to his own problems. The interviewer risks that the respondent may have no answers or may have answers other than those that the interviewer had in mind and that therefore, desirable change may not ensue.

A perceptive appraisal interviewer fits his interview style to the situation and to the specific individual in order to gain maximum understanding and produce a desire to change. He knows that a problem-solving style tends to create the least anxiety and defensiveness because subordinates tend to perform best when they have participated in setting their own goals for improvement. When the interviewee can recognize potential benefits and realize positive results from the appraisal interview, supervisor-subordinate relationships are improved.[17] Appraisal should be an ongoing practice rather than an annual ordeal that both supervisors and employees dread and too frequently forget as soon as it is over.

Should written evaluation forms be used, these should be given to the individual before the interview so that he has an opportunity to formulate a rebuttal or an explanation regarding his noted deficiencies. If we are using the appraisal interview to help people improve job performance rather than to trap them or "chew them out," this opportunity for reflective thought is very beneficial. The reasons that a situation persists and methods of changing that situation are what is important to the health of the organization—not simply pointing out the problem.

Opening Comments

In beginning the interview, clearly state the purpose and proceed immediately to the evaluation—which should be fully documented. Avoid generalities! The interviewer may start by asking how the individual reacts to the rating or what attitudes or behavior he demonstrated during the rating period that would justify the evaluation. The interviewer wants to discover why things are as they are and how they may be changed. Ideally, changes will be suggested by the interviewee, but if he does not provide them, the interviewer must request other behavior that will lead to more positive results.

[17]N. R. F. Maier, *The Appraisal Interview* (New York: John Wiley and Sons, 1958), pp. 22–25.

Internal Summaries

By summarizing each area where new action is agreed upon, the interviewer establishes a steppingstone for further solutions. These internal summaries also avoid confusion and disagreement and create a feeling of progress.

Changing Behavior

Thorough knowledge of the people with whom he talks enables the interviewer to determine his methods and also set priorities regarding behavior and attitudes that he wants modified—especially attitudes that directly affect behavior. For example, when an individual cleans his fingernails during a discussion, answers the telephone by saying "yep" or "ya," or calls his secretary or other women in the organization "Honey," indicate directly that his behavior is not acceptable and should be changed. On the other hand, when an individual is fractious in his conversation, late for appointments, or occasionally unprepared, there may be underlying attitudinal motivations for that behavior; in this case, the attitude must be modified in order positively to affect the behavior. Whenever the interviewer indicates that behavior or attitude has negative connotations, he should be able to cite persons, places, and dates to substantiate his observations and contentions. The interviewer should not discuss behavior that is unrelated to the interviewee's job performance or his relationship with other employees.

Closing Comments

In closing the appraisal interview, the interviewer should summarize the proposed action intended to effect change and leave the impression that communication is open. Should the interviewee feel that he has been incorrectly evaluated on certain items, ask him to write a note to that effect, if he chooses, that can be attached to the evaluation-summary in his personnel file. A follow-up conference in which the interviewer presents his final evaluation and points out goals for the next evaluation period will provide a meaningful developmental experience.

COUNSELING

The counseling interview is problem-solving in that its purpose is to help someone recognize a problem so that he can then deal with it. Such interviews, because of their extremely sensitive nature, should be conducted by experts, but they seldom are. Dressel observed:

It has been said that giving advice is like kissing; it costs nothing and it is a pleasant thing to do. While I do not believe that counseling is synonymous with giving advice, the analogy, nevertheless, has some relevance. Counseling has further similarities to kissing in that (1) everyone feels qualified to practice kissing and most everyone does it at sometime; (2) the objectives of kissing are really not clearly stated but are not entirely intangible; (3) kissing itself is apt to be so satisfying that there is little tendency to evaluate it otherwise.[18]

Recognizing the Problem

Some counseling interviews start by soliciting information; this leads to a statement of a problem; and the interviewer then suggests action to solve the problem. Other approaches, notably those suggested by Carl Rogers, propose only to assist the client in recognizing his problems so that *he* may develop desirable means of dealing with them. In the latter forms of counseling, the interviewer never attempts to impose his values or ideas; the approach is completely respondent-centered, involves listening, observing, and clarifying, and is nondirective. Action results from the client's conscious desire to change.[19] Problems beyond the normal ones of cooperating with others, changing assignments within an organization, and developing approaches to solving problems should only be handled by well-trained psychologists and psychiatrists.

Counseling interviews are usually requested by the client. Every effort should be made to set an appointment time that gives the interviewer the opportunity to learn as much as he can about the individual and to discover how functional the individual is within the organization. The interviewer should try to learn the nature of the specific problem, if possible, before the actual interview.

A Receptive Environment

A good counseling interviewer knows how others perceive him; he is aware of the verbal and nonverbal behavior that he can affect to encourage a positive reaction. He is always receptive and "always available." During the interview, he avoids telephone calls and other interruptions and gives the client his complete attention. He allows the individual time to complete the interview, or if time constraints are imposed by his schedule, he arranges for a follow-up interview so that all business may be completed.

[18]P. Dressel, "The Evaluation of Counseling," *Concepts and Programs of Counseling,* ed. R. Berdie (Minneapolis, Minn.: University of Minnesota Press, 1951), p. 70. Reprinted by special permission of The Univ. of Minnesota Press.

[19]A. N. Turner and G. F. Lombard, *Interpersonal Behavior and Administration* (New York: Free Press, 1969), pp. 298–299.

It is extremely desirable to establish a receptive environment in which free conversation will flow. Greet the respondent at the door; make him comfortable; provide an ashtray so that he may smoke. The interviewer should not sit behind a desk unless he wishes to enhance his authority; nor should he place any other physical barrier between himself and the person he is talking with. Even though you may anticipate the reason for the interview, allow the individual to state clearly why he is there. Although most counseling interviews are requested by the interviewee, in some instances the interviewer initiates the session; if such is the case, state clearly at the beginning of the interview why the request was made. In the opening comments, don't rush. Take plenty of time to establish rapport and achieve common ground. A counseling interviewer with a reputation for fairness and confidentiality has already made considerable progress toward dispelling the negative feelings that many individuals have about the counseling situation. The client who believes that he will be heard, and not judged, by a sympathetic individual, often looks forward to the opportunity of "sharing his burden" with someone else.

EFFECTIVE TECHNIQUES

When the client has requested the interview, allow him to begin talking about whatever interests him most; do not push directly to the problem. What troubles him may be painful, embarrassing, or humiliating. His small talk and the interviewer's sympathetic listening will soon lead to a statement of the principal problem.

Control the Situation

In conducting the counseling interview, view all comments, no matter how seemingly irrelevant, as important. Avoid becoming emotionally involved and thereby expressing attitudes which may be viewed as judgments. Defer comments other than those that promote continued response from the interviewee. Such comments as "yes," "go on," and "what happened next?" are sufficient stimulation for the interviewee to continue talking. Occasionally reflective or mirror questions, in which the interviewer restates or rephrases what the interviewee has said, may promote further discourse. When the interviewee uses gross language because he is emotionally disturbed or because he wants to control the situation by shocking the interviewer and putting him on the defensive, the best reaction is no reaction at all—unless such behavior is uncontrolled.

Nonverbal signals expressed through posture, eye contact, and vocal force and timbre, provide valuable clues to the counselee's emotional condition and influence the interviewer's reaction to language. When the interviewer recognizes that he is being intimidated, he may reasonably express the opinion that the session has deteriorated and suggest that in order for the session to continue, the gross language must cease. Control is necessary for continued progress, and at times it can only be achieved through firm assertion.

Appropriate Questions

Sometimes the counselor, in his desire to help, may press the client with too many questions. The counseling interview is not a cross-examination; avoid asking so many questions that answering them prevents a client from expressing his true feelings and ideas.[20] Questions that help the client look more deeply into his problem and think for himself serve as stimulation, direction, and motivation—when time is permitted to thoughtfully contemplate the answers. Argumentative questions, sermonizing, and extensive probes into embarrassing incidents are clearly detrimental.

Directive Response

Ideally the interviewer will motivate the interviewee to solve his own problem. Should this not be possible, the interviewer might then suggest specific action or point out possible consequences of failure to change. For example, he might say, "Since we both agree that you are having trouble budgeting your time, let me suggest that for a week you time each of your daily activities so that we can discover exactly how you are using your time. This information may provide a foundation for reordering your priorities." Or the interviewer may say, "Since we both agree that this plan is inadequate, it seems clear that if you don't come up with a different plan—one that is acceptable—we will either have to give the assignment to someone else or replace you in the organization." Let me stress that these highly directive responses should be used only when other nondirective approaches have failed.

Concluding the Interview

The closing of the counseling interview is very important because the final impression that the interviewer leaves with the interviewee will either encourage or discourage further communication. Don't be in a hurry to get the person out of the office, and don't introduce new topics when a course of action has already been proposed. It is appropriate to say, "I think we've accomplished a lot in this conversation, and I sincerely look forward to

[20]Benjamin, *op. cit.,* pp. 77–88.

talking with you again.'' Some small talk (completely unrelated to the topic discussed) as the interviewee is walked to the door adds much to the feeling of good will and openness that are so desirable in a counseling relationship.

Note taking or recording of the interview is not advised. Write a summary of the interview from memory immediately following the counseling session, and place it in the personnel file. Present law allows the counselee access to that file.

PERSUASIVE INTERVIEW

The persuasive interview attempts to change behavior by means other than threats and compulsion. Persuasion is most effective when a need for change is demonstrated, when such change is consistent with the interviewee's ability, when change can be demonstrated as feasible, when the benefits of change can be clearly demonstrated, and when no other course of action is available. Clearly the interviewer must know as much as possible about the interviewee in order to make his own language and behavior most appealing and thereby avoid unnecessary conflicts and contradictions that interfere with his purpose.

Establish Reputation

The most persuasive interviewer is one who has established a reputation for credibility through his attainments, character, and experience. This reputation is enhanced when the persuader is confident, poised, eventempered, alert, and energetic in the presentation of his material. The effective persuasive interviewer has carefully analyzed the events that have led up to the interview and has appropriately prepared the interviewee by furnishing advance material so that certain common understandings exist at the very beginning of the interview. He makes an appointment for the interview at a time and date when he believes the interviewee will be most relaxed and receptive. The interviewer is thoroughly prepared with statistics, testimony, research, and examples to support all facets of his proposal. A single weak point—one that is unsupported—can be detrimental to the total persuasive situation.

Achieve Agreement

From his analysis of the interviewee, the interviewer knows that there will be certain items upon which both agree. He should begin with these. He should never be reluctant to concede a point, especially if it is not directly related to the final issue and certainly if hostility can be avoided. By first stressing the areas of agreement, it is much easier to deal with disagreement should it arise. The interviewer who presents an unbiased view of *both* sides of an issue before pointing out the advantages of accepting his contentions is generally thought to be unbiased, and his credibility is enhanced.

Effective Tactics

Questions in the persuasive interview are used to encourage active participation, to obtain overt agreement, to challenge generalizations, and to clarify attitudes, feelings, and facts. In short, questions in the persuasive interview furnish valuable feedback on which to base further argument. The key to persuasive interviewing is syllogistic reasoning—a way of arriving at conclusions based upon a major and a minor premise. For example, if the problem is a lack of efficiency in the personnel department, the persuader begins by getting agreement that change is productive—the major premise. He next presents a plan that will modify the operation of the personnel department—minor premise. His arguments in the minor premise are directly related to an agreement he has achieved—that change is desirable. He concludes logically that when his plan is adopted, efficiency will increase.

The interviewer may structure his support of the minor premise through induction or deduction—using examples, either hypothetical or real, cause and effect, or mere assertion, depending upon his relationship with the interviewee and his knowledge of the subject. The successful persuasive interviewer makes the complex seem simple, provides relief from frustration and anxiety, sometimes by offering a scapegoat, and appeals to the respondent's ambition and pride. He is able to redirect the respondent's basic motives and desires to conform with his own. These tactics are presented with the understanding that all persuasion is for a good purpose!

Elicit Action

The interviewer concludes the persuasive interview by summarizing the points of agreement and obtaining a commitment for action. This action may be as simple as setting a date for further discussion; it may involve appointing an *ad hoc* committee to furnish further information; or it may result in an assignment to "put the plan into operation" or to purchase a product.

The ideal interviewer is an individual who is thoroughly prepared—through research and analysis of the topic and the interviewee; one who can communicate his preparation and interest by being a sympathetic listener and by asking and answering appropriate questions; he is perceptive and skilled in the art of discourse. The good interviewer is a sensitive, considerate helper and friend.

WRITE
TO BE READ

Chapter Eleven

Most of this book has dealt with language and visual signals as they relate to oral presentation; however, it seems appropriate to devote a final portion to consideration of written reports. Reports are the essence of most management communication systems because they furnish much of the information upon which decisions are made. Unfortunately too many reports are poorly written, dull, and ponderous; some are unintelligible and confusing; and a few are vague and disordered to the point of being useless. Good reports are difficult to write; the report writer must have a thorough knowledge of his subject and his reader, a strong sense of logical order, and a good command of the language used. He must be willing to write and rewrite until he has defined his purpose and supported his contentions with the most pertinent information arranged in the clearest, most logical form and directed to the idiosyncrasies or particular demands of his reader.

Control Anxiety

Most report writers do not write because they want to; they write because their job requires it. Because writing is a difficult and sometimes painful task, it is frequently postponed to the point at which pressure causes anxiety, and the anxiety frequently results in a spewing out of all data in a series of unrelated and inconsistent statements. When the procrastinator has put all his information on paper, he stops writing—pleased that he has met one more deadline, even though he may have contributed nothing of value.

The trauma of report writing can be overcome when the writer knows what he is expected to do and has developed techniques for accomplishing that task. The manager who has established a climate in which good writing is expected and recognized will find increasingly that reports submitted to him have substance and value.

Effective reports are produced when the writer and the reader have agreed upon a set of standards for the composition and its evaluation. The writer must consider the reader's experience, education, specific responsibilities, and interests, and the purpose of the information requested.

Many reports are inadequate because the reader did not make his needs clear; sometimes the writer, because of vested interests or personal preference, disregards those needs. Reports are frequently weakened by the writer's reluctance to report facts or conclusions that he believes will be unpleasant to the reader.[1]

Meaningful Feedback

When a manager discovers that reports are unsatisfactory and returns them to the writer for revision, he should fully inform the writer of the specific deficiencies and furnish some guidelines for satisfactory completion of the assignment. Writers become discouraged and demoralized when a draft is returned with no indication of why it was unacceptable. A report returned to the writer with only the comment "unsatisfactory," by discouraging initiative and increasing frustration, results in productivity.

The monthly or weekly report that is filed marked "unread" should be eliminated. Efficiency requires that reports be requested only when needed and that they be read so that appropriate feedback can be given to the writer. Reporting for the sake of reporting creates useless paperwork when the manager or subordinate could be doing something more important; it also leads to carelessness and indifference.

Good writing must be encouraged by pointing out ways of improvement as well as deficiencies in composition and research. Every worker needs to be listened to; positive reaction is the principal motivation for continued achievement. Recognition of good efforts leads to better reporting. Therefore, a firm management practice must be to furnish appropriate feedback about all major reports.

[1]*How to Increase Office Efficiency and Cut Costs* [Special Report by the Capitol Bureau of Business Practices]. rev. ed. (Englewood Cliffs, N.J.: Prentice-Hall, 1960), p. 29.

Develop a System

Good report writing requires more than a knowledge of the subject and an acquaintance with grammar and syntax. William Gallagher delineates ten basic steps in preparing and writing a report. The completion of each step leads clearly to the next, and therefore none should be skipped in haste to meet a deadline. One can be reasonably sure he has adequate content in his report when he begins by:

> (1) stating the problem clearly; (2) defining the scope of the study; (3) planning the research; (4) collecting appropriate information; (5) analyzing that information; and (6) as a result of analysis, form conclusions and recommendations.
>
> To insure that the content has logical form, the writer then (7) organizes the report, (8) writes the first draft, (9) revises that draft at least once, and (10) presents the report to the reader.[2]

with the expectation of appropriate feedback and resultant action if necessary.

Information may be gathered from a variety of sources including colleagues, but the responsibility for the conclusions and the final report is the writer's alone. Reputations in organizations are, in large part, made by reports, so a system that insures appropriate collection of data and a method of arranging that data in the most forceful sequence and the best form is essential. Gallagher's sequence includes appropriate controls that enable the writer to correct deficiencies and meet defined standards.

Define Terms

Just as definition is the keystone for understanding in oral presentations, so is it in report writing. Different people accord different meanings to words because of their background, experience, environment, and perhaps their age or sex. A good report clearly defines the meaning of words in context, not only so that the boundaries of the investigation may be identified but also so that the focus of the report is clearly delineated. Scope and focus depend on the writer's knowledge, organizational objectives, or both. Vague, abstract instructions result in ambiguous reports. Because time, budget, availability of information, and other factors may limit the scope and focus of a report, these should be clearly defined for the writer so that he may furnish the most pertinent detail in the final presentation.

[2]W. J. Gallagher, *Report Writing for Management* (Reading, Mass.: Addison-Wesley, 1969), p. 14.

Collect Information

In report writing, planning simply classifies and divides into workable units the scope of the investigation. Planning also makes research less time-consuming because it focuses specifically on recognized problems. Planning assists the writer by suggesting what information is needed, where to look for it, how to collect it, and when sufficient information has been gathered.

All research used to support conclusions, whether taken from secondary published sources or primary sources, such as interviews, should be carefully documented.

Establish Validity

Once information has been gathered, it should be analyzed for its validity—i.e., to verify facts and to establish relationships between the various parts in order to create a meaningful whole.

After the analysis the writer uses his judgment to reach conclusions and make recommendations regarding the solving of a specifically stated problem. He presents evidence to support his conclusions, and these are based upon a clear recognition of organizational values and needs and stated in precise management terminology.

Outline

Organization of content provides focus, direction, and impact. All principles of organization regarding oral presentations apply equally to written presentations—with the additional caveat that written communication requires greater conciseness. The nonverbal, interest-maintaining signals used by a speaker are, of course, absent when a report is read. Therefore, other techniques must be employed to assure that a report receives the attention that it deserves.

Summarize

A good report starts with a summary or abstract of the principal conclusions; this may motivate the reader to study the body and appendices, especially if he is skeptical about the conclusions. A good report also avoids discussion about the difficulty of gathering material, any lack of cooperation among the writer's colleagues, and any other reasons that the report may not have met the specifications of the assignment. Opening comments describe why the study was conducted, what aspects were considered, what was discovered, and what action should ensue. Extensive background material is generally unnecessary, the manager knows why he made the assignment and what he hopes the report will prove. The report begins by winning confidence and establishing rapport with the reader—perhaps even playing upon his preconceptions and prejudice regarding the subject.

Support Conclusions

The body of the report expands upon and supports the conclusions, with the sections of the body appearing in the same sequence in which conclusions are stated in the introduction or summary. Such an arrangement makes it easy for the reader who wishes to examine the support for only one conclusion. The body of the report should also incorporate the logic and cohesion used to formulate conclusions.

The psychological advantage of arranging the body of a report in the journalistic "inverted pyramid style"—that is, starting with the most important elements and listing in descending order the support for those conclusions—is that the support then uses a flashback technique that reinforces the conclusions already planted in the mind of the reader. This arrangement also highlights the results of the analysis and may stimulate interest in reading further. It implies that the summary or final conclusion should be prepared before the supporting material is written, so that the summary has the same function as the outline does for oral presentations. You may use in written presentations the same arrangement of ideas and supporting confidence in their ability to express themselves; they may feel that they lack

The First Draft

Once material has been gathered and organized, the writer can begin the first draft. At this point doubt and delay usually occur. Many writers have great difficulty in putting the first word on paper because they lack confidence in their ability to express themselves. They may feel that they lack the necessary knowledge, precision in composition, or worthwhile ideas. When these doubts occur, the writer must review the information gathered and the outline to determine whether he has indeed focused on the purpose of the report. If so, the writer need not fear that he will lack clarity.

A carefully prepared outline permits the writer to begin the actual writing with any section of the report, and once he has completed one section, the next usually comes easier. Having organized and completed smaller sections of the report, he has only to tie them together with appropriate transitions. Begin writing with the section that is easiest to compose, and then move on to the next most difficult. This does not eliminate the writing of extremely troublesome parts, but it does build confidence and relieve pressure because by the time that you reach those parts, you are aware that you have already completed a good portion of the report. Finishing portions of the report serves as motivation for finishing the whole report. The initial draft of the report should be written quickly and with lit-tle attention to mechanics, syntax, or choice of words; the writer can refine in the second or third draft. The purpose of the first draft is to get as many ideas on paper as quickly as possible. It is a working paper whose flow and momentum should not be interrupted in order to polish.

When composing the first draft, minimize distractions. Close your of-fice door and instruct your secretary not to interrupt. If you cannot work on the draft in the office, take the work home or arrange with your superior to absent yourself from your office while you compose. The writer should be rested and his mind free from troubling intrusions. Most people know the time of day and circumstances when they work best; it is under these condi-tions that they should write reports.

Personally I prefer to dictate first drafts. This helps me resist the temptation to revise immediately because I cannot see what I have dictated until it has been typed. Having been a speech-and-theatre teacher for many years, I also feel that I am more fluent when speaking than when writing. This is true for many people. Oral language seems to have greater simplicity, clarity, and enthusiasm than written language. When ideas are expressed simply and directly in a first draft, it is much easier to establish proper rela-tionships between them in a revision. Regardless of the method of writing a first draft, it is the revision of that draft to which the writer brings unity, coherence, and emphasis.

Revise

If possible, write the first draft quickly and then put it in the desk for a day or two before attempting to revise it. Second thoughts are often better crystalized than first thoughts; second thoughts are critical while first thoughts are creative. A second reason for not revising immediately is that having just composed the report, the writer may be so pleased to have finished a difficult task that he may not readily recognize redundancies, ir-relevancies, and inconsistencies—which will be apparent and easy to eliminate after a brief interval away from the work. All writers are pater-nalistic about what they have written, and time away from the report will provide the necessary respite that permits dispassionate judgment.

When revising any work there are several questions the author should ask: Does it tell the story? Are the conclusions substantiated? Is the em-phasis correct? Is the information pertinent and accurate? Is the material presented logically? Is there clear definition of terms? Is the report easy to read and free of illiteracies? And, finally, is it directed to the needs of the reader?

It is especially in this latter light that all revision should be done. Writers write for someone else, not for themselves! I have found that by reading aloud, I can more easily decide what is appropriate, clear, and meaningful than by silently reading and re-reading a sentence. Sometimes the eye betrays us, but when the sentence is orally articulated, its faults are more obvious.

Be Concise

In any report conciseness is of paramount importance; it saves time by maximum use of every word and phrase. Conciseness eliminates irrelevancy and discourages self-indulgence and apology.

The concise report is free of unnecessary repetition, verbosity—principally caused by overuse of descriptive adjectives—and circumlocution. It avoids the dead wood of vocational jargon and unnecessary prefixes and suffixes that often rob perfectly understandable words of their intended meaning and make communication awkward and pretentious.

When expressions are used to indicate that what follows is important, the importance should be explained or the expression eliminated—for example, when one says, "It is important to note. . . ." When the importance of something is not fully explained, such expressions do not strengthen the impact of an idea; they weaken it. By eliminating the unnecessary, the writer may be reasonably assured that the reader will take the time to read the report properly—provided, of course, that it was necessary in the first place.

Be Clear

Conciseness may occasionally be sacrificed to clarity. Sometimes a report lacks sufficient explanation; this invites misinterpretation. If the reader does not understand, he may take no action or, worse still, the wrong action. Clarity demands conciseness but also selectivity in arranging words and phrases and in incorporating appropriate and pertinent detail.

Lack of clarity may also result from an inadequate vocabulary, a desire to equivocate, or a propensity to write in general terms for fear that precise expressions will invite precise criticism. A good report writer avoids the use of abstract terms and euphemisms because these lack precise meaning.

Clarity comes from appropriate qualification. For example, if the data are incomplete or if a judgment is founded upon assumption, the writer should indicate that. The problem with qualification is that it usually becomes over-qualification because writers wish escape clauses so that they will not be held fully responsible should the conclusions be unacceptable. Excessive caution in report writing produces frequent use of "approximately," "generally," "probably," and "roughly." These "hedge words," when used to modify a statement, communicate to most readers an inept analysis, faulty perception, or lack of self-confidence. In all instances such modifiers weaken the impact of the statement and obscure meaning.

The good report is free of jargon, which at best has snob appeal only to the few initiates who understand it.

The writer can reduce ambiguity by employing the active voice. It is also helpful to clearly define or eliminate conjunctions with more than one meaning—for example, "while," "since," and "for." Be careful about placing the modifiers of a noun after it rather than before.

Notice how the placement of the adverbial modifier changes the meaning of the following sentences:

1. I *only* am speaking tonight.
2. *Only* I am speaking tonight.
3. I am speaking *only* tonight.
4. I am *only* speaking tonight.

Misplaced phrases can cause confusion. For example, note the difference between "The director appeared to discuss his new plan *at the meeting*" and "The director appeared *at the meeting* to discuss his new plan." The latter sentence is concrete and explicit; the former invites interpretation.

Clarity may be enhanced by using Arabic numerals instead of connectives in a series— as in "Production will be increased by: (1) astute selection of new personnel, (2) retraining of present employees, (3) clearly outlined objectives, (4) periodic evaluation of achievement, (5) managerial feedback."

Paragraph Development

Paragraphs are used to develop a specific idea. The sentences in it lead from one thought to the next and support a final conclusion. The length of the paragraph depends upon the complexity of the idea and the qualifications of the reader. There is really no uniform size to a paragraph, although most single ideas can be developed adequately in seventy-five to two hundred words.[3] By varying the lengths of paragraphs, the writer can subordinate less important material and emphasize the more important. A paragraph that differs significantly in length from those that precede and those that follow it commands attention and emphasizes the idea that it contains. Variety in the paragraph length is desirable in order to maintain interest.

Paragraphs are not a series of unrelated statements. Good paragraphs

---

[3]*Ibid.,* p. 132.

usually consist of a first sentence that presents the main idea (the so-called topic sentence), followed by developmental statements, and a final sentence that evaluates, reviews, or gives the rationale for what is presented in the body of the paragraph. Because many readers scan only the first and last sentence of each paragraph, these are the statements that must be most carefully structured.

The body of the paragraph may be developed through definition, analogy, comparison and contrast, example, statistics, cause and effect, question and answer, historical perspective, or mere assertion. All material contained in development should be relevant to the topic sentence and support the conclusion. Form and technique emphasize content.

Correct Grammar

Correct grammar is important because it makes writing easier to read and suggests a writer's competence and knowledge of his material. Errors in standard grammar and spelling may imply a careless research and fuzzy logic, and thereby diminish the reader's confidence in the writer. Correctly or incorrectly, the writer's ability to spell, punctuate, and use proper syntax frequently gives the reader an indelible impression of his preparation, intelligence, and competence. The better a writer understands and observes the rules of grammar, the more confidence he has in his ability to construct clear, logical sentences and paragraphs. Such confidence will be repaid in the positive feedback given the report.

Style in Presentation

The presentation of clear, concise, complete, and accurate information will not assure readability if the presentation lacks style. Style influences attitude and enhances meaning; it gains and maintains attention. Weller Embler contends that "style is not ornament, or virtuosity, something superfluously added to a simple meaning; it is the meaning."[4] Style connotes a mastery of material and the ability to state something in a compelling way. Style has a quality of naturalness, vividness, and spontaneity which is tempered with discipline and technique. It has a sense of pace, tone, variety, imagination, and harmony. Style, more than any other element of writing, reveals the personality of the writer. It is style that enhances, brightens, and makes excellent thoughts interesting and acceptable.

[4]W. Embler, "Style Is as Style Does," *E.T.C.: A Review of General Semantics* 24 (1967): 450.

THE SEMBLANCE OF STYLE

Chapter Twelve

The successful manager and the aspiring executive must clearly possess the professional qualifications for their positions. They also have discovered that when competence is reinforced by appropriate behavior and appearance, leadership and influence are more easily obtained.

A large portion of this text is devoted to techniques for developing effective managerial behavior, including communication. A significant element, and one that is easily controlled, is the manager's appearance. Careful grooming, appropriate clothing, and an office that is tastefully designed and furnished to reflect his personality are forms of communication that an executive can definitely control.

THE OFFICE

When the manager has a choice of location, he should choose a space as close to the chief executive office as possible but one that is also readily accessible to subordinates.[1] A manager's office should be divided into a business area, where the desk is located, and a conversation area furnished with a coffee table, comfortable chairs, and possibly a couch. Strive to

[1]A. DeLong, "Dominance-Territorial Relations in a Small Group," *Environment and Behavior* 2 (1970): 170–190.

make the division of areas appear natural rather than contrived. Use the window in an office to frame the desk. Should a window not be available, then appropriate drapes, wall hangings, or a painting should be used as a backdrop for the executive desk.

Metal desks and office furniture have certain unfavorable connotations associated with bureaucracy. However, when only metal furniture is available, a glass writing surface and other carefully selected items placed discreetly on the desk communicate a more favorable impression. A wooden desk should be functional but not so large as to dominate the room and the person sitting behind it. The executive chair should have a leather or cloth cover that blends with the office decor. Two visitors' chairs should be available—one at the side of the desk for more intimate conversation and one directly in front of and facing the desk situations in which the manager wishes to stress his authority.

The office should convey efficiency, planning, and purpose; therefore, unless you absolutely must have immediate access to filing cabinets and coatracks, these should go in the secretary's office. To add to a feeling of efficiency, display in the bookcase only those books that are frequently used. Most managers prefer a relatively uncluttered desktop, choosing rather to keep materials in a credenza with drawers that is located behind the desk. Wooden floors should be covered with area rugs, which help to delineate the different functions of the office. Floors in poor condition should be repaired or covered in wall-to-wall carpet.

The best wall colors for a business office are eggshell, beige, or a very light orange, blue, or yellow. These colors have positive psychological connotations and are not aggressive or threatening in their implications.[2] One wall may be painted a rich color or covered with woven bamboo, wood paneling, or grasscloth; the additional texture of this wall will provide richness and variety. Keep bulletin boards, charts, graphs, and other business visuals off the walls. When such materials must be used for a meeting, place them on a portable easel. All furnishings should be arranged so that the occupant of the office is the instant visual focus for anyone entering the room.[3] The office must be a visual, functional tool—a symbol of the authority, creativity, and influence of its occupant.

The waiting room creates an especially good first impression when on the walls are paintings and prints, when carefully selected periodicals and newspapers are current and in good condition, and when the office secretary demonstrates by demeanor and appearance that you have a dignified, efficient professional colleague and managerial assistant.

[2]M. Luscher, *Color Test,* trans. I. A. Scott (New York: Random House, 1969), pp. 9-19 and 34-50.

[3]N. Russo, "Connotations of Seating Arrangement," *Sociometry* 28 (1965): 337-348.

THE WARDROBE

In addition to arranging the physical environment, the manager can influence those with whom he comes in contact by choosing a wardrobe that reflects what many people consider good taste and upper-middle-class achievement. Dress cannot compensate for incompetence, but incorrect dress can definitely be detrimental to upward organization mobility and the acceptance of ideas.

People wear clothing for protection and modesty and to make a good impression on others. The impression that male managers most want to convey is one of authority, responsibility, masculinity, friendliness, and power. The way a person dresses does indeed affect his credibility with certain groups and his acceptance by many organizations.[4] An individual's environment affects his behavior, and the clothing that one chooses becomes an intimate part of that environment because it influences and motivates reactions from other individuals.

The Business Suit

When choosing a suit color, stick with blue, gray, and beige and avoid green and very light blue, which lack authority. A black suit should be worn only by a manager in an extremely authoritative position or by a small man who wishes to increase his authority. Dark brown suits suggest the lower middle class, are drab, and should be avoided unless chosen for a very specific audience.[5]

Material of very narrow pinstripe makes an extremely desirable business suit, especially if the suit has a vest. Chalk stripes are somewhat less desirable, and suits with them should be conservatively tailored. Chalk stripes tend to be gaudy, and on a very heavy or a very thin person they can suggest deviant behavior and suspicious motives.[6]

Some plaids make acceptable business suits if they are carefully coordinated with the appropriate shirt, tie, and socks. For business purposes, avoid the large, flashy patterns frequently used for sport coats. Wool herringbone and other tweeds, in dark blue or black and tan shades, make extremely desirable business suits, because these materials definitely symbolize the upper middle class. Garish sport jackets and high-fashion suits of French or Italian style should be saved for sportswear and evening dress.

[4]J. Mills and E. Aronson, "Opinion Change as a Function of the Communicator's Attractiveness and Desire to Influence," *Journal of Personal and Social Psychology* 1 (1965): 73–77.
[5]J. T. Malloy, *Dress for Success* (New York: Peter H. Wyden, (1965), pp. 41–50.
[6]N. H. Compton, "Personal Attributes of Color and Design Preferences in Clothing Fabrics," *Journal of Psychology* 54 (1962): 191–195.

Double-breasted suits should be worn only by thin men. Heavy men look better with side vents in the coat; thin men are more attractive with the center vent in the back of the jacket.[7] Conservative camel hair and dark blue sport coats worn with matching solid or soft plaid slacks offer an acceptable alternative to the business suit. Attractive sweaters, matched for ensemble effect, are sometimes acceptable—especially for the junior executive or the senior manager who in certain situations wants to signal a softer attitude.

Proper Fit

A well-fitting suit appears to have been tailored for the wearer alone. Trousers must fit properly at the waist, seat, and crotch. Trousers with plain bottoms should be cut one-half inch longer at the back than the front. When cuffs are chosen, they should be no more than one-and-one half inch wide, and the trouser bottom should hang so that it is exactly horizontal to the ground and just brush the toe of the shoe. The vest must be fitted closely to the body to avoid wrinkles and sagging. The jacket sleeves should be five inches from the tip of the thumb. The jacket should fit properly across the shoulders and behind the neck; it should be free of lumps or bulges. If it does not fit, insist that it be altered. Try the suit for fit both standing and sitting. Use *your* judgment, not the salesman's, about how the suit looks on you. If necessary, see a fashion consultant before you shop and have him check the fit before you buy.

Psychological Values

Large men have the advantage of seeming to be more authoritative, but they occasionally overwhelm others simply by their size. To minimize distractions and inferiority feelings in others, large men should avoid dark colors and severely tailored suits. They should also avoid pinstripes and vests. Medium-soft grey and beige suits are best for the large individual, who should also avoid strong color contrasts and any accessories or neckties that call attention to his already authoritative appearance. He should also avoid excessively heavy shoes.[8]

Conversely, the small man can add to his stature by wearing pinstripe suits with vests, Ivy League ties, and white shirts. His outer garments should be heavy and luxurious; a camel hair or dark blue cashmere is best. A snap brim hat goes well with these coats. Small men who seek increased authority should use such attention-getting accessories as a handkerchief showing from the breast pocket of the suit jacket, an expensive wristwatch, and large cuff links. Glasses with heavy frames also tend to give authority to the

[7]Malloy, *op. cit.* pp. 48–50.
[8]P. N. Hamid, "Some Effects of Dress Cues on Observational Accuracy, a Perceptual Estimate and Impression Formation," *Journal of Social Psychology* 26 (1972): 279–288.

countenance of the small or extremely thin man. Precision and neatness in dress are great advantages for the small man in establishing authority.[9]

In no enterprise other than academia is the disheveled or sloppy look tolerated. Men elsewhere who have a "dumpy" or "lumpy" body—who, no matter how hard they try, do not look well in clothes—must be as neat as possible, with hair combed, nails manicured, and shoes shined. Neatness and effort can compensate heavily for what nature did not provide and clothing cannot conceal.

Coordinate for Effect

Regardless of a man's size, his clothing must be coordinated in terms of color, line, texture, and style.[10] It is important not to wear a horizontally patterned tie with a pinstripe suit or a light silk tie with a heavy tweed suit. A pinstripe suit worn with a plaid shirt is as inappropriate as a narrow string tie worn with a wide-lapel double-breasted suit. Wearing a dark suit with a dark shirt and dark tie is as gauche as combining a green shirt, red tie, and yellow suit. In the first example, the colors would make the countenance of the individual seem too pale, and in the second, the colors are so incompatible that they would dominate the individual.

Accessories: Shirts

Shirt material with a shiny look or a see-through weave is suitable for sportswear, but keep these out of the business office. Soft cotton shirts of good quality offer the best look for the business executive. Cotton shirts require careful laundering, starching, and ironing. A good shirt fits around the waist, with no bagginess or bunchiness, but it is also loose enough to allow one to sit without having the buttons pop open. One that is too loose diminishes the manager's impression of power, while one that is too tight suggests sloth by emphasizing the flesh above the collar. The shirt tails should be long enough to remain snugly tucked into the trousers. The shirt should fit precisely at the collar and should have at least seven buttons, including the collar button. A manager who is older, with wrinkles in his neck, should wear high-collared shirts, occasionally even turtlenecks. All shirt sleeves should terminate just below the wrist bone, about one-half inch below the jacket sleeve.[11]

White and solid-color shirts are the most acceptable for business; they are also much easier to coordinate with any style or color of suit. Striped shirts are acceptable if the stripes are not more than a quarter-inch

[9]*Ibid.*
[10]R. S. Greene, "Accentuate the Appropriate," *New York Times Magazine,* Part 2, September 18, 1977, pp. 40–45.
[11]Malloy, *op. cit.* pp. 51–68.

apart. Stripes should be worn only with solid-color suits unless the coordination with patterned garments is very carefully and delicately done. Multicolored stripes should be avoided because they are very difficult to coordinate with tie and suit and are less authoritative. Plaids may be worn when the pattern is extremely delicate and when the colors are closely coordinated with the suit and tie. Plaids are generally associated with sporting events and other outdoor activities but may be absolutely appropriate and advantageous when worn in certain selected situations.[12]

Short-sleeve shirts tend to have a lower-class or middle-class stigma; they are appropriate only for after-office activity or company outings where the manager wishes to give the impression that he is "one of the boys." If one must wear a short-sleeved shirt, he should never remove his coat.[13]

Ties

Suits, shirts, and ties should be purchased at the same time in order to coordinate colors, style, texture, and line. It is wise to buy two or three shirts and at least two ties for each suit.

John T. Malloy contends that "the tie is probably the single most important denominator of social status for a man in the United States today." It is a "symbol of respectability and responsibility . . . it reinforces or detracts from [people's] conception of who you should be."[14] The tie adds "class" to the clothing ensemble.

When a tie is knotted properly, the tip comes just to the top of the trousers. The tie width should be in keeping with the style of the suit and should never be wider than the lapel. The Windsor knot is satisfactory for silk or other light material, while the four-in-hand, or half-Windsor knot, is more appropriate for heavy material. The thoughtful manager wears a bow tie only with formal dress or at after-business sporting events. When a tie becomes soiled, have it cleaned immediately; if it becomes wrinkled, have it pressed; when it becomes worn, discard it. This class symbol must be impeccable.[15]

Solid-color ties coordinate well with any patterned suit or shirt. The polka-dot tie also goes well with almost any shirt or suit if the dots do not pick up the color of the shirt; the club tie, with selected sport emblems displayed upon a solid background, is a good variation of this style. The regimental ribbed or corded tie is a favorite of American businessmen. This diagonally striped tie should be of dark colors carefully coordinated with your other clothes. Ivy League and paisley ties tend to be sportier in style

[12]R. Hoult, "Experimental Measurement of Clothing as a Factor in Some Social Ratings of Selected American Men," *American Sociological Review* 19 (1954); 324–328.

[13]*Ibid.*

[14]Malloy, *op. cit.* p. 7

[15]*Ibid.,* pp. 69–87.

and therefore have certain limitations; however, these ties may be worn with dark-colored suits to achieve a striking effect. The difficulty, of course, is that such patterns do not contribute a serious tone to the clothing ensemble. Plaid ties convey the least authoritative impression.[16]

Shoes

Black, brown, and cordovan are standard colors for business shoes; highly polished patent leather should be avoided. A wit once commented that "men in white shoes always look like tourists." Plain-laced shoes, wing tips, and dress boots and loafers are acceptable—provided that they do not have large metal buckles or tassels. Please, no wing tips with flaired trouser legs! Socks should cover the calf, with sufficient elasticity to avoid drooping; solid colors are preferable.

Grooming

Well-cut, well-combed hair helps create a neat, efficient managerial look. Most men in authority tend to be conservative; they do not like the crew cut, "white sidewall" look, or overly long "mod" hairstyle. How one likes his own hair is irrelevant; what is important is how those who make judgments about management perceive the wearer of that style. An extremely short haircut may convey an impression of lower-middle-class status and values, but it can also suggest a desirable athletic or military background. Extremely long and highly styled hair may indicate inordinate self-interest and frivolous purpose. Blacks should avoid the extreme "Afro cut" because of its political implications among some members of society. These are the generalities; the best course is to adopt a hairstyle that is acceptable in the manager's own organization and circumstances.

THE FEMALE MANAGER

Women are generally more aware of fashion, fabric, and style than are men, but here are a few suggestions for the female manager.

My impression has intensified during the past few years that female managers are growing increasingly bored with the concept that they must dress like men in order to be accepted as managers in a "man's world." A woman who has accomplished something in her job and who feels confident that she is competent is likely to resent the insinuation that she needs to disguise her femininity by wearing tailored suits and matronly shoes. Most women want to wear something that is attractive and comfortable, fits her

[16]*Ibid.*

managerial and lifestyle, and looks natural. More than men women tend to seek individuality in their dress; they want to escape from the business uniform.

There are, however, some nonverbal signals regarding apparel that female managers can adopt that will prove beneficial in their relationships with men and with other women in business. A tailored gray, dark blue, or black suit with a skirt is the most acceptable and reliable outfit for the female manager. Pant suits, tailored skirts and blouses, and conservative dresses in unpatterned fabrics are also acceptable for variety. A well-pressed pleated skirt suggests neatness and precision. Avoid stretch and polyester fabrics; they become misshapen and baggy and therefore tend to diminish your influence. Vests are harsh and masculine—even though they may accentuate the bustline.

Long-sleeved blouses of white silk, polished cotton, or broadcloth are best if they are finely tailored, with a minimum of lace and frill. A dark, solid blue, black, or deep red blouse also adds an authoritative complementing color to a suit ensemble.

Women may effectively wear a blue, tan, or gray blazer with either a tailored skirt or tailored slacks. Removing the blazer—if the blouse is long-sleeved and cuffed—does not have the same negative effect as a man removing his coat. Slacks and skirts should be properly lined and fitted; they should not be so tight that the undergarment line shows. Except at very informal meetings, the female manager should avoid a sweater-and-slack ensemble—which conveys a casualness that may diminish other people's sense of her seriousness of attitude and purpose. High-fashion cocktail and after-dinner dresses are inappropriate in a business office.

Flesh-colored stockings or pantyhose project a much more serious and mature image than do mesh stockings or stockings of various shades and hues. The latter should be worn only if a woman wants to attract attention to the part of her anatomy encased by these garments. Such diversions may diminish, or at least modify, the quality of verbal discussion. Women should avoid flat-heeled shoes; although these suggest casualness and comfort and allow for easy mobility, they cause a woman to walk and stand in a way that makes her appear less attractive and commanding than when she is wearing shoes with heels. The ideal shoe is a simple, closed-toe pump, with moderate heel, suitably colored (black, brown, blue, gray) to match the ensemble.

Do not wear a man's necktie! This kind of signal is aggressive and threatening, especially to many older male colleagues. An appropriate soft ascot or scarf is adequate to adorn the blouse; an open collar is also becoming and tasteful—if no more than two buttons are open. A matching handkerchief in the lapel pocket will add authority to the tailored suit without being obtrusive. Jewelry chosen carefully—small earrings, simple bracelets, perhaps a modest gold or silver chain or a string of pearls—adds a nice polishing touch to a suit or dress. A watch, with a face large enough to readily reveal the time, signals that the female manager is schedule-conscious and serious.

The female manager should avoid immoderate makeup. Lipstick and blushes or light rouge are sufficient for most business occasions. As a woman gets older, she may wish to add panchromatic makeup in order to soften or obscure wrinkle lines, but she should avoid heavy eye shadow and eyebrow pencil. The best makeup looks like no makeup; it does not call attention to itself but rather accents the pleasing features of the person.

A female manager should not wear long, flowing hair below her shoulders or over her face, and she should never adopt a piled-high lacquered, shiny hairdo that says, "I just came from the hairdresser." Such extreme hair styles connote inordinate self-concern and a lack of propriety, and will be distracting as the female manager conducts her daily business. Most female managers have their hair trimmed above the collar, either in soft, flowing waves or in a Dorothy Hamill-athletic look. Regardless of the style chosen, wear your hair soft and full; avoid a masculine look.

A female manager should never wear a fur coat or any other high-fashion outer garment to the business office or on a business trip. A camel hair wrap-around or a cashmere blue, gray, or tan full-skirted coat with appropriate belting that does not pinch at the waist is best. A very short coat or cape transmits less positive signals. Leather coats suggest a "macho" attitude; they are better for sports occasions than for business transactions. Tan and dark blue are the best colors for raincoats. Wear only brimmed hats or female fedoras; save other, more highly styled, chapeaux for social occasions. Choose tightly fitting leather gloves of brown, black, or gray, suitable matched to the outer garment.

If you must carry an attaché case, carry one that looks as though it belongs to you—one that fits the size of your body and matches your wardrobe. Handbags should be of high-quality leather, free of gaudy buckles and other ornamentation, and the leather should not shine.

The female manager's lingerie should be of sufficient quality and fit to hold her breasts firmly in place without revealing entirely the contour of her body. Pantyhose or "underalls" that do not reveal the lingerie line through the outer clothing are preferable. In no case should the lingerie be of a color that contrasts with or shows through the outer garments. This may be desirable and attractive in certain social situations; it is inappropriate in business.

Many of the suggestions directed to male managers about the psychological values implicit in form, style, and fabric are equally applicable to the female manager.

FINAL WORDS

The importance accorded to appearance is justified when we recognize that people make moral and value judgments about others based on their dress and grooming. They make similar judgments about the quality of the organization with which these individuals are associated. First impressions *are* important. The competent manager who does not have the semblance of competence, which is immediately recognized in his appearance, has a communication barrier to overcome. Why start with a disadvantage—especially one that is easily overcome! An impression of efficiency, reliability, and energy can be conveyed, at least in part, by the precision and taste of the office and by the coordinated clothing and neatness of the manager.

NOTE ON TRUSTWORTHINESS

Appendix

I. Definition:
  - A. *Trustworthiness* is the manifestation of the competence and character of the speaker insofar as these attributes tend to influence the acceptance or rejection of his statements and proposals.
  - B. The speaker's trustworthiness is also affected by the authorities he cites, such as prominent speakers, writers, or institutions (newspapers, universities, etc.)
  - C. The speaker must also deal with the trustworthiness of his opponents, present or absent, persons or institutions.
  - D. Trustworthiness of authorities may be dealt with on the same basis as trustworthiness of the speaker.

II. There are three components of trustworthiness:
  - A. *Competence:* general or specific: ability, training, opportunity to observe.
  - B. *Moral integrity:* sincerity, honesty, dependability; the "good man."
  - C. *Good will* toward audience: the speaker has no selfish motives, but shows interest in the good of the group.

III. Manifestation of trustworthiness may be:
    A. *Negative:* absence of manifestation; no attempt by speaker directly or indirectly to influence audience as to trustworthiness of himself or his authorities.
    B. *Favorable:* Manifestation of character making audience tend to accept.
    C. *Unfavorable:* Manifestation of character, or a challenge by opponent, making audience less inclined to accept or more inclined to reject.

N.B. Obviously it is to the speaker's advantage to point up the favorable trustworthiness of himself and his authorities and the unfavorable trustworthiness of his opponent and opposing authorities. Such procedure does not involve deceiving or misleading the audience.

Trustworthiness also depends on the speaker's reputation before he speaks, and on what is known about his authorities, etc.

IV. Reactions of audience related to trustworthiness:
    A. As to statements of fact:
        1. Generally *negative* where the information is readily available, known to be available to the speaker and also to anyone who might want to check up on the speaker. (E.g., areas, population, distances, statistics as to distribution in clear-cut categories, such as occupation, historical events, etc.)
        2. *Competence* of speaker or authority needs to be established where the facts are difficult to get at. (E.g., special investigations or experiments, happenings in out-of-the-way places, very recent happenings, etc.) Lack of competence, especially specific, is unfavorable.
        3. Unfavorable where audience detects deliberate distortions of facts.
    B. As to statements of opinion:
        1. *Competence* needs to be established. For young speakers authority is usually needed: "I think" is largely useless. (E.g., as to what was the cause of some situations; what result some action will have, etc.)
        2. *Moral integrity,* usually of authority, may need to be established in recommendation of action, especially for some audiences (e.g., religious). Lack of moral integrity is very unfavorable.
        3. *Good will,* especially absence of selfish interest in outcome, may need to be established. Selfish interest is very unfavorable.

INDEX

Active listening, 36-39
Adaptors, 25
Ad hoc committees, 13, 120
Age, barriers caused by, 53-57
Aggression, female, 52
Ambition, lost, 56-57
Anticipation, listening and, 40
Appearance, 30-32, 47, 163-72
Appraisal interview, 143-46
Appreciation, job performance and, 4-5
Aristotle, 80
Arms, communication with, 23-24, 50
Associated Country Women of the World, 46
Attitudes:
    of audience, 89
    conflict of youth and age, 54
    to physical environment, 29
    public speaking and, 70
    sexist, 46-47
Audience, 70-73, 75-82, 84-92

Bach, G.R., 115-16
Basil, D.C., 46
Beebe, Steven, 22
Behavioral models, 71-73
Bierbaum, Eugene, 121
Blair, Hugh, 123

Body movement, 23-25
Body types, 32
Brainstorming, 123
Breath control, 98
Brownell, Judi, 51
Butler, K.F., 103

Cannell, C.F., 133
Cash, W., 125, 129, 136, 142
"Chain of command" communication
    system, 3
Chairman, committee, 120-22
Character traits, leadership, 105, 107
Circular response, 8-9
Clarity:
    in public speaking, 76, 92-93
    in report writing, 159-60
Clothing, 31-32, 165-72
Coalition of Labor Union Women, 46
Coherence, speech, 81
Committee reports, 121
Committees, 120-23
Communication:
    barriers (*see* Communication barriers)
    "chain of command" system, 3
    control, 85
    cultural, 36

Communication *(cont.)*:
feedback, 4, 9-11, 14, 20, 47
group discussion (*see* Leadership and
    group discussion)
informal, 3
instructional, 7-8
interpersonal, 3, 26, 48, 52, 125-29
managerial, 3, 5
motivational, 8
network, 6, 9, 10
nonverbal (*see* Nonverbal communication)
organizational, 8, 9
public speaking (*see* Public speaking)
rap sessions, 12
rumor, 13-14
systems, 7-14
telephone, 11-12
Communication barriers, 2, 38, 39, 43-68
age, 53-57
language, 61-64
race (*see* Race)
sex (*see* Sex)
Competition, 12-13
Complexion, 64
Conboy, William, 5
Conciseness, in report writing, 159
Conclusions, in report writing, 157
Conferences, 121
Confidence, 69-70
Conflict, handling, 115-20
Confrontation, 52
Control, 14-15, 85
of interviews, 127-29, 148-49
listening and, 39-41
Conversation, 66
Counseling interviews, 146-50
Courtesy, 126
Crawley, J.E., 46
Cultural awareness, 35-36
Cultural communication, 36
Cultural influence, 19-21

"Dead wood," 54-55
Defensive behavior, 51
Delivery, in public speaking, 91-103
Dewey, John, 113, 118, 127
Dialogue, 122
Directive interviews, 130
Discrimination, reverse, 59
Discussion group (*see* Leadership and group
    discussion)
Distance, converstion and, 28
Downs, Calvin, 140
Dressel, P., 146-47
Dyad, 125-29

Eakins, B.W., 49
Eakins, R.G., 49
Ectomorph, 32
Effect displayers, 25
Ekman, Paul, 24-25
Embler, Weller, 161
Emotional reinforcement, 21-22
Emotional response, 38, 62-64
Empathy, 25
Emphasis, in speeches, 81
Employment interview, 140-43
Endomorph, 32
Entertainment, public speaking and, 76, 77,
    91-92
Equal opportunity, 59
Ethnic perspectives (*see* Race)
Evaluation, listening and, 39-41
Eye contact, 22-23, 25, 27, 28, 30-31, 34,
    50-51, 65, 66, 95

Feedback, 4, 9-11, 14, 20, 47, 154
Feedback agent, 10-11
Female assertion, 51-52
Female managers, appearance, 169-72
First draft, in report writing, 157-58
Follow-up, 143
Forum, 122
Freedman, J.L., 50

Gallagher, William, 155
Gatza, J., 144
Generalization, 38
Gesture, 18-19, 23-25, 31, 95-97
Gillette, William, 73
Goals:
    discussion, 108, 109, 112
    organizational, 5
    of speeches, 76-77, 79
Good will, public speaking and, 79
Gordon, P.J., 46
Grammar, 161
Grievance officer, 9
Grooming, 169
Group leadership (*see* Leadership and group
    discussion)

Hall, Edward, 26
Hanawalt, N.G., 71
Happiness, job performance and, 4-5
Horne, Patrice, 27
Humor, in speeches, 78

Illustrators, 24-25
Impressions, instant, 20-21
Informal communications, 3

Information:
  sharing, 8
  in speeches, 76
Information gathering interviews, 137-40
Instructional communications, 7-8
International Business and Professional
    Women, 46
Interpersonal communication, 3, 26, 48, 52,
    125-29
Interviews, 1, 125-51
  appraisal, 143-46
  control of, 127-29, 148-49
  counseling, 146-50
  courtesy in, 126-27
  dyad, 125-29
  employment, 140-43
  information gathering, 137-40
  organization of, 135-36
  persuasive, 150-51
  purposes of, 137-40
  qualities of interviewer, 131-35, 139
  questioning, 132-36, 138, 149
  special considerations, 129-30
  techniques, 142, 148-51

James, William, 96-97
Jealousy, 54, 56
Job performance, 4-5
Job security, 5
Johnson, Lyndon Baines, 112

Kahn, R.L., 133
Kindall, A.F., 144
Kinesthetics, 24-25

Language:
  barriers caused by, 61-64, 67
  public speaking and, 85-90
  sex barriers and, 48-50
  signals, 37-38
Leadership and group discussion, 105-23
  character traits, 105, 107
  committees, 120-23
  corrective measures, 120-23
  decisions, 107-8
  factors of influence, 109-15
  goals, 108, 109, 112
  handling conflict, 115-20
  style, 107-9
  subordinates, 111
  tenets of, 105-9
Lecture-forum, 122
Legs, communication with, 23-24, 50
Lei, T.-J., 76
Leviton, T.E., 46

Listening, 35-41
  active participation, 36-39
  control and evaluation, 39-41
  cultural awareness, 35-36
  emotional response, 38
  generalization, 38
  language signals, 37-38
  nonverbal signals and, 36-37, 39
  note taking, 39-40
  reaction time, 39
  selective, 40
Listening profile, 41
"Looks and Glances" (Ogden), 30
Luscher, Max, 110

MacGregor, Douglas, 6-7
Malloy, John T., 168
Managerial communication, 3, 5
*Managerial Situations and How to Handle
    Them* (Wachs), 54-55
Martin, Robert, 140
Mehrabian, Albert, 18
Memorization, 73
Menopause, 45
Menstruation, 45
Mesomorph, 32
Metaphor, 37-38, 86
Miller, G., 108
Mintz, N., 110
Monczka, R.M., 44
Monroe, Alan, 113, 118
Motivation, 8, 41, 44 (*see also* Leadership
    and group discussion)
Movement, 18-19, 23-25, 95-97
Myths:
  of racial superiority, 59-60
  about women, 44-46

Newstrom, J.W., 44
Nichols, Ralph, 36
Nondirective interviews, 130
Nonverbal barriers to communication, 64-66
Nonverbal communication, 17-34, 36-37, 39,
    41, 50-51, 66, 94, 110, 148
  body movement, 23-25
  cultural influence, 19-21
  emotional reinforcement, 21-22
  empathy, 25
  eye contact, 22-23, 25, 27, 28, 30-31, 34
  gesture, 18-19, 23-25, 31, 95-97
  perception, 30-34
  proxemics, 26-30
  trust, 21-22, 24
  values, 22-26
Nonverbal interaction, 25-26
Note taking, 39-40, 139

Odor, 32, 33
Office, 163-64
Ogden, Arthur, 30
Ombudsman, 9
"Open door" policy, 11
Openness, 3-4
Oral communication (*see* Public speaking)
Organizational chart, 3
Organizational communication, 8, 9
Organizational goals, 5
Organizational health, 5
Outlines:
    report writing and, 156
    speeches and, 77-78, 80, 82-83, 103
Overconfidence, 70

Panel, 121
Paragraphs, in report writing, 160-61
Perception, 30-34
Personal touch, 4
Persuasion, 76-77
Persuasive interviews, 150-51
Planning, 14-15
Platform behavior, 91-103
Power games, 58
Presentation style, in report writing, 161
Problem solving, 1, 112-14, 122-23
Proxemics, 26-30
Public speaking, 60-103
    audience, 70-73, 75-82, 84-92
    behavioral models, 71-73
    breath voice, 98
    clarity, 76, 92-93
    confidence, 69-70
    delivery, 91-103
    good will, 79
    ideas, organizing, 75-84
    language, 85-90
    memorization, 73
    movement and gesture, 95-97
    overconfidence, 70
    persuasion, 76-77
    preparation, 69-84
    rehearsal, 72, 94, 101-3
    rhetoric, 87, 88
    speech voice, 97-101
    stage fright, 70-73
    style, 85, 88-90, 103
    timing, 100-101
    topics, 75-76, 77
    trustworthiness, 173-74
    vocabulary, 86-87
Punctuality, 31, 33, 65

Questioning, 132-36, 138, 149
Quinn, R.P., 46

Race, 57-68
    language and, 61-64, 67
    myths, 59-60
    nonverbal barriers, 64-68
    power games, 58
    racism, 57-58, 67-68
    reverse discrimination, 59
    stereotyping, 60-61, 67
    values, 67-68
"Racial" space, 65-66
Racism, 57-58, 67-68
Rap sessions, 12
Reaction time, 39
Reefe, W., 44
Regulators, 25
Rehearsal, public speaking and, 72, 94,
    101-3
Relativity, meetings and, 29
Report writing, 153-61
    clarity, 159-60
    conclusions, 157
    feedback, 154
    first draft, 157-58
    grammar, 161
    outlines, 156
    paragraphs, 160-61
    presentation style, 161
    revision, 158-59
    summaries, 156-57
    system, 155
Resistance-to-new-people syndrome, 55-56
Response, 20
Revision, report, 158-59
Rhetoric, 87, 88
Risk taking, 6-7
Rogers, Carl, 147
Role playing, 123
Rosenfeld, Howard, 48
Rumor, 13-14

Safe distance, 27
Sargent, F., 108
Seating arrangements, 27, 28-29
Selective listening, 40
Self-image, 47-48
Self-perception, 2-3
Semantics, 61-62
Sensitivity, 1, 15
Sex, 30, 43-53
    attitudes, 46-47
    confrontation, 52
    female assertion, 51-52
    language and speech, 48-50
    myths, 44-46
    nonverbal signals, 50-51
    self-image, 47-48

Sex *(cont.)*:
    sexism, 46-47, 48, 51-52, 53
    stereotyping, 43-44, 53
    values, 43-44
Sexism, 46-47, 48, 51-52, 53
Sex object, 49
Sex roles, 43-44
Shaw, G. Bernard, 89, 93
Silent Messages (Mehrabian), 18-19
Space control, 27
Spatial design, 30
Spatial relations, 26-27
Speeches:
    audience and, 70-73, 75-82, 84-92
    body of, 78, 80-83
    coherence of, 81
    conclusion of, 78, 84
    elements of, 75
    emphasis in, 81
    entertaining, 91-92
    goals of, 76-77, 79
    humor in, 78
    information in, 76
    introduction of, 78-80
    memorization of, 73
    orientation in, 79
    outlines of, 77-78, 80, 82-83, 103
    preparation of, 75-84
    topics of, 75-76, 77
    unity of, 80
Speech voice, 97-101
Stage fright, 70-73
Standing committees, 120
Stereotyping:
    race, 60-61, 67
    sex, 43-44, 53
Stuart, C., 125, 129, 136, 142
Subordinates, leadership and, 111
Summaries, in report writing, 156-57
Supportive environment, 3-7

Symbols of achievement, 32
Symposium, 121
Syntax, 62

Table talk, 27
Tape recorder, 72, 139
Telephone, 11-12
T-groups, 123
"Theory X—Theory Y Model for
      Management Motivation," 6-7
Thorensen, Paul, 116
Timing, in public speaking, 100-101
Topic outline, 82-83
Touching, 33, 64
Trust, 21-22, 24
Trustworthiness, public speaking and, 173-74

Unity, of speeches, 80

Values:
    racial, 67-68
    sex role, 43-44
    signaling of, 22-26
    of youth and age, 54
Videotape recorder, 102
Visual code, 24-25
Vocabulary, public speaking and, 86-87

Wachs, William, 54-55
Winthrop, Henry, 54
Working models, 1-15
    communication systems, 7-14
    planning and control, 14-15
    self-perception, 2-3
    sensitivity, 1, 15
    supportive environment, 3-7
Written reports (*see* Report writing)
Wyden, P., 115-16